C000172039

My Dad's Cortina

First published in May 2009

British Library Cataloguing in Publication Data:
A catalogue record for this book is available
from the British Library

ISBN 987 184425 696 9

Library of Congress catalog card no. 2008943646

Published by Haynes Publishing, Sparkford,
Yeovil, Somerset BA22 7JJ, UK
Tel: +44 (0) 1963 442030
Fax: +44 (0) 1963 440001
E-mail: sales@haynes.co.uk
Website: www.haynes.co.uk

Haynes North America Inc.
861 Lawrence Drive, Newbury Park,
California 91320, USA

Design and layout by Richard Parsons

Printed and bound in the UK

Acknowledgements

The majority of the pictures and illustrations in this
book are drawn from the Giles Chapman Library with
the exception of the main photo on page 77, reproduced
with permission of Rex Features (with thanks to Stephen
Atkinson), the upper photo on page 84, reproduced
courtesy of Kudos Film and Television, and the main
photo on page 85, reproduced by permission of
Fremantle Media (with thanks to Jane Foster).

The author would also like to gratefully thank Fiona
Pargeter, John Nevill and especially David Hill at Ford
Motor Company for assistance and location of specific
pictures; literature suppliers Andrew Currie and Pooks
Motor Books; Graham Robson; Neill Bruce; Derek Smith
and Mark Hughes at Haynes Publishing; and dads – mine
and yours – everywhere, for making the Cortina a British
institution that's been enjoyable to research and salute.

My Dad's Cortina

OTW 325D

Giles Chapman

Contents

Archbishop approacheth

If you could get hold of a copy – and, even today, it's a highly confidential little dossier – then *The Red Book* would make fascinating reading.

Was it actually red? Who knows. Did it even exist in book form? Hard to tell. But one thing's certain: like many other mythical documents containing everything from the recipe for Coca-Cola to the on-line machinations of Google, it contains the formula for a cultural phenomenon. In *The Red Book*'s case, it holds the secrets of the Ford Cortina's astounding impact on the British motoring scene.

Compiled in three-and-a-half months in 1960, it's a detailed list of every single component to be used in the Ford Cortina Mk I that was launched two years later. Dull as it may sound, this data was absolute dynamite when it came to creating a sales winner. The design team had looked at parts used in other successful cars and, in every case, worked out how they could be made better and cheaper. Famously, they had bought a Mini, taken it to pieces, and realised the British Motor Corporation must be losing about £30 on each car it built; less well-known is that they held the slide rule up to the Volkswagen Beetle too.

Armed with *The Red Book*, Ford could then know exactly how much every part would cost to make, and how much it would weigh.

But it you feel this must be a rudimentary lesson from the School of the Blindingly Obvious, think on. Back in 1960, this method of 'product planning' was startlingly new. Most carmakers, believe it or not, worked on the basis of hunch: they built what the managing director, of even the ageing founder, deemed right, and many thought analysis was a dirty word.

Ford had employed its first product planners at its Dagenham headquarters in 1953. In those days, it made economy cars like the Anglia and Prefect and a range of larger saloons, the four-cylinder Consul and six-cylinder Zephyr…and none of them was especially inspiring, efficient or profitable. The 1959 Anglia 105E, with its natty styling and peppy engines was deservedly popular, but a slightly bigger brother,

Opposite: the four Cortina generations that ruled Britain for 20 years; below: the natty Anglia 105E

Above: Consul Classic – dud; opposite: 1962, Montlhery circuit, Paris, and Ford executives try Cortina and Taunus 12M against rivals

the 1961 Consul Classic intended to fill the gap between the Anglia and the bigger Consul, was a disaster with its tacky styling and a leaden performance thanks to its heavy, Forth Bridge-like structure. Even before it arrived in showrooms, Ford knew it was a dog.

In those days, Ford's various global outposts – thanks to historic agreements and the interference of governments – were surprisingly self-contained, but on a trip to Detroit in 1960, Ford of Britain's chairman Sir Patrick Hennessy discovered some dismaying news: Ford's usually lacklustre German offshoot was working on an alarmingly promising new car.

In fact, what was already codenamed as 'Cardinal' had originally been designed in Detroit as an ultra-compact model to slot in below the Ford Falcon. Instead, that project was axed and the whole shebang gifted to Ford Germany in the company's

continuing policy of assistance as the war-torn country was rebuilt; it promised a tasty shoe-in to mainland European markets.

The worst of it was, the Cardinal packed the sort of new technology that would shame Dagenham's products, and especially the dreadful upcoming Classic. It had front-wheel drive, a compact, space-saving V4 engine, and neat, timeless styling. Hennessy's arse was on the line, not to mention Britain's pride and can-do attitude. Something had to be done, and fast.

Soon after touching down from America, Hennessy summoned his chief product planner Terence Beckett and executive engineer of light cars Fred Hart. From the urgency of that gathering sprang *The Red Book*, with its obvious focus on the front-drive Mini and German standard-setter the Beetle. "Ford of Germany is going to make the Cardinal. I want to beat that. You've got only two years", commanded Hennessy.

And to lift morale, the car they needed to create – an entirely new generation of popular British Ford that every self-respecting dad must yearn to own – would have its own codename: 'Archbishop'. Hennessy chose it to get one up on the Germans in the religious pecking order. Only later did they discover 'Cardinal' had been named after a bird found widely in North and South America, and that, depending on interpretation, an archbishop didn't always out-rank a cardinal anyway!

Nonetheless, the Cortina seed was sown.

In super-quick time, Ford's design team, *Red Book* to hand, set to work on the 'Consul 225'. It

would be a car for Britain's new motorway era so, as well as pulling in the pound notes for Ford's accountants and pleasing US honchos, it would need to be light yet gutsy. With all these vital factors in mind, the car broke new ground in having its body structure designed using aircraft engineering stress technology: the body engineer Dennis Roberts had previously worked at the Bristol Aeroplane Company.

Later to become chairman of Ford in Britain, and knighted for his role as 'Mr Cortina' by a grateful nation, Sir Terence Beckett recalled:

"We decided we needed a bigger body shell and we also needed more wheel movement. We decided that we would provide a proper boot – in a way, we overdid that, but it was perfect for a 'rep' who wanted to take samples, and perfect for the family motorist. The Cortina came in under cost and, most significantly, we did it in record time. We took just 21 months from full-size clay style to Job 1 – which was then an all-time record for the industry".

But working on 'Archbishop' was also the making of Alex Trotman, later Lord Trotman and eventually chairman of the Ford Motor Company mothership in the USA. His concern, from the day in 1955 when he began work as a 22-year old management trainee in the purchasing department, was the methodology by which Fords were manufactured and sold at a profit. The details of the first component he had to chase never left him: "It was the radiator of the old Consul. It was E5PD2. When you could be fired, you're inclined to remember things like that".

It proved an invaluable training ground for team member Hamish Orr-Ewing, too – he eventually

Opposite: original Consul offered no new tricks; above: Cortinas today in Ford's Heritage Collection

became chairman of Jaguar in the mid-1980s. "We originally began to think of a 'new Prefect', which would fill a gap between the Anglia 105E and the existing Consul Mk II – in size, performance and price".

But what really made the new car hit the ground running was the partnership between engineer Fred Hart and an ebullient Canadian Ford stylist drafted in to help, Roy Brown. His prime task was to establish a proper design department at Ford – in fact, he tasked young British designer Charles Thompson with shaping 'Archbishop' – but Brown was in overall charge of melding Italian-influenced styling simplicity with a sparing touch of Detroit glamour. Not an easy trick to pull off, that, as the hideous Classic had amply proved. "We started with a blank page and we had a wonderful time with that car", said Brown later. "It was nice to see it become such a success". Turn the page to join the start of that successful story.

Nothing like a dazzling white
Cortina to set an eligible man apart;
that and a good head of hair

BUA 432C

The Ford Cortina Mk I

When new models are revealed for the first time, reaction from buyers is usually one of excitement tinged with annoyance; there tends to be an infernally long wait between the glittering unveiling and the time when customers can actually get their hands on one. Sometimes, a year can elapse between announcement and delivery. And that's very frustrating for a car-mad dad.

But not with the first Cortina. The cars had already been rolling down the production line for four months when, on 21 September 1962, they made their debut at Ford dealers' showrooms across Britain. It was an astounding feat of cloak-and-dagger logistics, because the launch still made a massive impact.

"The weekend we launched, every British dealer had 12 to 15 cars", remembers Harry Calton, a young Ford public affairs executive at the time. "Every dealer knew that by the next weekend they were going to get another 15".

It was an indication of the go-go-go nature of the entire Archbishop/Cortina venture. It had taken just 21 months (and a precisely-budgeted £13m) between the 'sign-off' of its styling to the very first car screeching out of Dagenham

in May 1962. And, from day one, there was a proper range of models to choose from – two- and four-door saloons in standard and De Luxe trim. So Ford factory bosses could crack open the Pomagne on New Year's Eve 1962 after having built 67,050 of the new cars, 50,000 of them for export.

Another matter demonstrating the on-the-hoof decision-making process characteristic of Archbishop was the car's very name. It was originally going to be, as the 'Consul 225', a sort of sub-brand of the bigger Consul series; then, a decision to offer a bigger engine option meant there would be a

Good cunsternoon, Afterble: daunting line-up of Mk I Lotus Cortina motorway pursuit cars, pictured in 1965

The Consul 225 regalia is still intact on this early 'Cortina' De Luxe

'Consul 255' too. However, even as Harry Calton was running his publicity photo shoot of very early cars in Scotland, the plan was torn up.

"I got a telegram saying there had been a late change. New badges – Consul Cortina badges – were brought up to Scotland. We then had to re-photograph as much as we could in just two-and-a-half days".

Eh? Cortina? Where did that spring from? The northern Italian ski resort Cortina d'Ampezzo was certainly vivid in the public imagination because it was the venue for the 1956 Winter Olympics. But using it on this new saloon was actually another two-fingered gesture to the Germans from Ford of Britain.

The front-wheel drive Ford 'Cardinal', which also went on sale in 1962 as the Ford Taunus 12M, was deliberately schemed to cash in on the sales possibilities of the new European Common Market that had been created in 1957 between Belgium, France, Germany, Italy, Luxembourg and the Netherlands. Although Britain wouldn't join until 1972, in 1962 the age of jet travel and cheerful European influences from the espresso to the tulip bulb was already luring dreary old Britain ever closer to the vitality and style of mainland Europe. Clearly, the Consul name alone, redolent of imperialist diplomatic circles, was dated and stuffy, and the Cortina tag oozed glamour.

Walter Hayes, in charge of Ford's Public Affairs department, said in 1962: "We asked the authorities in Cortina if they minded their name being used on a new Ford car. It wasn't until later that I discovered Cortina also means 'curtain' in Spanish!" Still, Ford tried to placate conservative buyers by calling the car the Consul Cortina, only dropping the prefix in 1964 when the car's sales supremacy was unquestionable.

In one important area, though, there was no confusion. The Consul Cortina offered a hearty dollop of car for the money.

The Cortina 1200 standard two-door saloon of autumn 1962 sold for only £573, which was much less than any other car in the 1.2-litre saloon class… even if a heater was a £15 10 shilling extra! It was a mere £34 more expensive than a feeble two-door Morris Minor, but a satisfying £52 less than a Volkswagen Beetle 1200.

Was it a better car than those two yardsticks? Most would say the Cortina was tinny by comparison

A red Cortina GT on an open road; the experience fuelled saloon car expectations for 1960s drivers

Per-production Mk I Cortinas (note Consul 225 insignia) roughing it, a left-hand drive export model to the fore and, of course, compared to Beetle, Minor and Ford Taunus 12M, it was utterly conventional in engineering terms – front engine, rear-wheel drive, re-circulating ball steering, independent front suspension by MacPherson struts and coil springs, a rigid axle at the back with half-elliptic leaf springs; *The Motor* magazine said, simply, it was 'devoid of technical frills'.

But the, ahem, sparing nature of Ford's approach meant the Cortina could offer commodious dimensions yet also be lighter. The roomy body offered previously unheard-of space for front and rear passengers, oddments, and luggage in that cavernous, boxy boot. Meanwhile, it was a lively and predictable car to drive, not underpowered in any way and with a pleasing, crisp gearchange; 30mpg was easily possible.

In fact, the whole car gave the impression of being the accomplished, latest evolution of the traditional saloon, not in any way groundbreaking but eminently refined for the sustained cruising speeds of modern roads. It was simple and, so, reliable. So, it was little surprise that, as the motorway network led to British business thinking in national terms, rather than local ones, the Cortina forged a path in the emerging 'company car' era. It quickly became the first choice for fleet buyers whose job it was to issue corporate wheels to sales representatives – like, perhaps, you very own ambitious father – for their tours of duty. As the Cortina range rapidly widened to offer a vast array of options, so the appropriate car could be accorded to rising

Ford's sleek, prototype turbine truck dwarfs seven Mk Is in 1964; spot the promising new idea

corporate buccaneers while keeping the entire fleet Cortina-centred, removing hassle from the fleet manager's life. And, of course, making Ford's Thames-side plant in Essex almost white-hot with activity as it struggled to meet demand. Indeed, over 260,000 Cortinas were sold in 1963, its first full year, massively beating Ford's 100,000 estimate. The final Mk1 tally in 1966 amounted to 1,013,391, making this the fastest-selling British Ford so far – and wildly profitable, because some four out of five Cortina drivers ended up with – at the very least – the more expensive De Luxe model sitting proudly outside their semis. To top it all, export sales hauled £250m into the British economy, so the Labour government that won a landslide election in May 1966 had reason to be especially grateful for the Cortina's stunning pulling power.

And they've built an estate to put us all in...

It's hard to convey, today, just how few and far between compact estate cars were in early 1960s Britain. During the previous dingy decade, station wagons tended to be either vans with windows or else ugly conversions by funny little backstreet tinsmiths. From the mid-1950s, there was the Morris Minor Traveller and the Hillman Minx and, er, that was about it until the somewhat larger Vauxhall Victor estate came along in 1959.

Pitched in the middle of these two camps came the Ford Consul Cortina estate in 1963, and it rapidly proved the ideally sized load-lugger thousands of British motorists – your dad, especially – really wanted. The rear seats folded flat with the boot floor; you certainly didn't always get that with rivals.

And for the 1.5-litre Super version, Ford tried to jazz up the utilitarian image with a look of the American suburbs. It sported prominent trim panels on its flanks and tailgate for a real Country Club touch.

It wasn't, of course, real wood like that on the Morris. The polished mahogany imitation was provided by thin plastic 'Di-Noc' appliqué while the pine effect frame was fibreglass. It was a gamble with British tastes that didn't quite pay off. After 18 months, the pretend timber was swapped for two-tone paint, and sales took off!

Timeline: The Ford Cortina Mk I

Toymaster Corgi (opposite) captured the country club mood perfectly with its miniature tribute to the Super estate (below)

May 1962

Assembly begins at Ford's Dagenham, Essex plant of the Consul Cortina in three forms: Standard, De Luxe with column-mounted gearshift, and De Luxe with floor-mounted gearshift; all of them feature the four-cylinder overhead-valve engine of 1198cc.

Ford gave the Cortina a rallying cry early on

Ford shrewdly recognised that the Cortina's lack of technical innovation could be compensated for by a macho image. So in 1963 it established a motor sport nerve-centre at Boreham, Essex to pitch the Cortina into the glamorous maelstrom of international rallying. Its first triumph was to send a Cortina Super driven by Eric Jackson and Ken Chambers from London to Cape Town, a trans-African journey it achieved in a record 13 days.

Ford also asked Cosworth Engineering to develop the high-output Cortina GT engine. Even in its tentative 1963 season, this car shone at 1.6-litre class level, taking third place overall in the Swedish Midnight Sun rally; outright victories soon followed.

In 1964, Vic Elford drove a Cortina GT to win the tough French Alpine rally. Then Kenya's Ford importer Peter Hughes's GT won the prestigious

East African Safari rally, with the 'works' GT team swiping the Manufacturers' team prize – a first for European-prepared cars.

Roger Clark's privately-prepared Cortina GT won the Scottish rally in 1964 and 1965. Cortinas also starred in those new Rallycross events your dad loved watching on Saturday afternoon telly.

Little wonder the Cortina was named 'International Car of the Year' in 1964 for motor sport achievement by Swiss motoring magazine *Auto Universum*.

September 1962

The two-door Consul Cortina makes its debut in Ford showrooms, starting at £573 on-the-road.

October 1962

The four-door Consul Cortina joins its sibling at British dealers, sharing the same wheelbase, engine and trim levels but starting at £639.

Roger Clark, co-driver Tony Mason and Cortina Mk Is made an unbeatable combo; opposite: a GT kicks up Safari Rally dust

January 1963

A frantic year sees the Consul Cortina Super expand the range with a more powerful 1498cc engine, bigger brakes, and less austere interior; standard equipment includes chrome body strips and wheel trims, and a heater.

'It's what's up front that counts'

Released in 1963, the comedy film *Call Me A Cab* seemed a turkey until it was hurriedly renamed *Carry On Cabby*, and then cinemas were packed. Perhaps the tagline 'It's What's Up Front That Counts' helped lure punters in to see this rollicking battle of the sexes.

Neglected wife Hattie Jacques sets up her own cab firm – Glam Cabs – in direct competition with husband Sid James's Speedee Taxis. His dreary London-style vehicles can't compete with her brand new fleet driven by scantily clad young women, including actress Amanda Barrie, later famous as Alma Baldwin in Coronation Street.

In what seemed an incredible publicity coup for Ford, those Glam Cabs were all Consul Cortina Supers. They even appeared on publicity posters, with their heart-shaped roof lights. But, actually,

for the ever 'careful' producer Peter Rogers, it was a fantastic freebie because Ford, once asked for help, pulled out all the stops. Publicity executive Harry Calton purloined every available press car to make a convincing 'fleet'.

Another notable cinematic Cortina Mk I moment occurs in the 1965 'Swinging London' comedy *The Knack – And How To Get It*, as Rita Tushingham, Michael Crawford and Donal Donally hitch a ride on a transporter load of saloons fresh out of Dagenham.

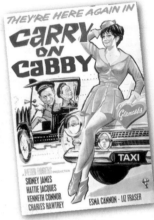

Not quite 'Carry On Cortina', but it might as well have been

January 1963

The bigger 1498cc engine can also be optionally ordered for the De Luxe.

January 1963

The Lotus-Cortina is announced with Lotus 1558cc twin-overhead-camshaft engine, coil-spring rear suspension and power front disc brakes, and aluminium doors, bonnet and boot.

BRITAIN'S NEWEST FILM STAR

—— THE NEW CONSUL CORTINA SUPER

The small car with a big difference

Some of the 'LOVELIES' with their Cortinas now appearing in the latest 'CARRY ON' comedy film.

CARRY on CABBY

SIDNEY JAMES · HATTIE JACQUES · KENNETH CONNOR · CHARLES HAWTREY · ESMA CANNON · LIZ FRASER

March 1963

The first Consul Cortina estate arrives, offered in De Luxe form with column or floor change and 1198cc engine, and also in distinctive Super form – featuring fake plastic wood trim – with the 1498cc motor.

How the interior blew away the opposition

Early Cortinas were mildly shocking when you opened the door and got inside. It was here that you could easily see the pared-down nature of the car's genesis, with acres of plain painted metal, a sparsely equipped dashboard, rubber mats on the floor, particularly spartan plastic upholstery, and a cheap-looking linear speedo.

It was, at least, exceedingly roomy. Then again, empty space didn't cost Ford a penny.

However, in 1964 came an innovation that made the Cortina's cabin just about the most inviting on the market. It was Aeroflow, the world's first controllable face-level fresh air ventilation system.

Memories of the extraordinarily cold winter of 1962 might still have been vivid, but driving on the newly opened motorways at sustained speeds was a horrendously stuffy business on sticky summer days.

Now Aeroflow, developed to perfection personally by Ford chief engineer Fred Hart, offered through-flow ventilation, sucking away humid air through vents in the rear screen pillars, and offered accurately responsive temperature control.

It was a vast improvement over any previous system, and soon widely aped by Ford's competitors. Families, and dads in particular, could now keep their cool no matter how terrible the delay…

April 1963

The 1498cc Consul Cortina GT – the world's first saloon car to wear this evocative moniker – packs 78bhp, stubby gearlever, sporty instruments, a Weber carburettor and front discs. It's offered as both a two- and four-door saloon, starting at £748.

The original and austere Cortina interior was made much less stuffy after Aeroflow ventilation (opposite) arrived

April 1963

The first Lotus-Cortinas are delivered to eager customers. Buying one sets you back £1100, and only 3301 are made.

Who's the daddy? The Lotus-Cortina sensation

Car enthusiasts were agog at the boldness of the idea – a family saloon given the 'works' treatment by Lotus? Blimey!

Apart from the twin-camshaft, twin-carburettor Lotus engine with 105bhp, this authentic hot-rod featured alloy body panels, cut-down front bumpers, wide wheels, and a white-and-green livery like a Dunlop Green Flash tennis shoe. Underneath were bespoke coil-spring rear suspension and front disc brakes.

The Lotus quickly grabbed the Cortina GT's mantle as Ford's race and rally headline-getter, its light weight, nimbleness and power proving a perfect formula.

In 1964, F1 World Champion Jim Clark took the British Saloon Car Championship, while Sir John Whitmore won five European fixtures.

Whitmore, nicknamed the 'Bearded Baronet', was synonymous with the Lotus Cortina's on-track antic of cornering with one front wheel off the ground.

In rallying, the Elford/Seigle-Morris Lotus-Cortina lifted the Handicap Category of the 1964 Tour de France, and Clark's Lotus-Cortina won the 1965 Welsh.

In Britain, these cars won their Saloon Championship class again in 1965, while in Europe Sir John Whitmore completely dominated the European Saloon Car series. Satisfyingly, a similar car won the British RAC Rally. It was much the same story in 1966, where Whitmore swiped four more outright victories in Europe, and Jim Clark three in Britain. In North America, if a Lotus-Cortina was beaten, it was invariably by V8-engined Ford Galaxies.

September 1963

After a full year on sale, all Consul Cortinas receive new circular instruments in a binnacle above the steering column, a self-lubricating chassis and doors that close with less of a hollow clang.

The Lotus-Cortina's furious race and rally outings saw Ford's image lift off as never before

October 1963

Ford reveals the Consul Corsair, a Cortina-based model to replace the Consul Classic. Filling the thin chasm in the Ford range between the Cortina and the Zephyr 4, it uses an elongated Cortina floorpan and Cortina Super engine, and is built at Halewood, Merseyside.

The Kent engine, central to the Cortina's success

The basic engine in the first Cortina made its debut in 1959 in the 997cc Anglia 105E, Its development codename was 'Kent', and it reinvigorated the company's small cars because it was Ford's first overhead-valve power unit, finally consigning its wheezy old sidevalves to history.

In 1962, a livelier, enlarged 1198cc version arrived in the Anglia Super and the Consul Cortina simultaneously. The in-line four-cylinder had the original's 80.96mm bore but with a stroke enlongated from 48.41mm to 58.17mm to increase capacity. It was rev-happy, and had 50bhp on tap.

An even bigger 1498cc edition appeared in the Super, offering 62bhp, which was then upped to 78bhp in GT tune.

Its five-bearing cast iron block formed the basis of the Lotus Elan engine, the iron head substituted for a new light alloy twin-camshaft one, and the capacity bored out to 1558cc. Completing a splendid circle, this was subsequently re-installed in the Lotus-Cortina.

Kents enjoyed an incredible 44 years powering countless Fords. A new crossflow cylinder head design arrived in Cortinas in 1967 for the Mk II, and the engine was later adapted for front-wheel drive to power the first Fiesta and even the Ka. Every spanner-wielding Cortina dad knew it well, but only after electronic ignition arrived in 1986 did the Kent unit lose its main bugbear – an exasperating reluctance to start on damp mornings.

December 1963

The Consul Cortina becomes more restful to drive with the first availability of a three-speed Borg Warner automatic gearbox option, for 1.5-litre cars only (but not the GT).

The inner workings of
Ford's Cortina-powering
'Kent' engine (left) laid bare
in this cutaway drawing;
the engine had an amazing
44-year lifespan

THEO PAGE F.R.S.A. U.S.I.A.

Those 'CND' rear lights and other styling matters

In its most utterly basic 1200cc form, the Cortina was a very plain looker, especially at the front with its grim, five parallel-bar grille and absence of chrome on anything but the bumpers.

But along the side of the car, the fluted design and flattened tail fins made all Cortinas seem super-sleek.

The styling was masterminded by Roy Brown, the Canadian previously responsible for the looks of Ford's ill-starred Edsel. But he tasked a young designer called Charles Thompson with creating the actual Cortina shape.

"This was my first ever whole-car assignment", Thompson later recalled, "but the side flute along the flanks was all down to Roy Brown; I spent a lot of time juggling with the position of that.

"We were originally only to do a two-door saloon – so when the four-door version was proposed, we literally had to fit the different doors and windows into the original envelope".

At the rear, the Cortina's tail lights, so evocative of the Campaign for Nuclear Disarmament's 'Ban The Bomb' logo, made the most impact, There was no mistaking a Consul Cortina to motorists travelling in its wake.

"We were going to have neat strips of angled lamps, and the body tooling was well underway", said Charles Thompson. "Then there was a last-minute change of mind, and the circular lamps were adopted".

September 1964

A relatively quiet year for the range draws to a close with the deletion of the word 'Consul' from its title.

Dust clouds would be the only fall-out from a Cortina GT, which was still ideal for the nuclear family

September 1964

A restyled mesh grille now includes sidelights and amber indicator flashers, and a heater and electric screen washers are now fitted to all but Cortina Standard models.

The uniquely dreamy Cortina of Stirling Moss

'Stirling Moss's flair for design and push-button living is almost as well known as his driving ability', declared *The Motor* magazine in October 1963. 'His association with Ogle to produce a practical "dream" car was a step that gladdened a great many motorists. Moss, they thought, would show them how it ought to be done'.

Hmm, right. Stirling must have been a restrained dreamer, because there was something rather pointless about the totally new back end with its 'notch back GT styling', which, while svelte, was pretty tame. Nifty new grille, though, with its inbuilt driving lamps.

Still, practical features abounded, like a rear screen wiper, interior boot release, reversing light (this was 1963, remember), a cassette tape recorder for music-playing or dictation, and bolt-on hubcaps 'to obviate prising and marking' – dads could relate to that one. Convenience goodies included electric windows, a Hobbs automatic gearbox, and opening quarter-lights front and rear, while shiny touches like chrome gearlever, aluminium steering wheel and a Webasto sunroof put on the Ritz.

A thrifty car to carry four people for 500 motorway miles in comfort was Moss's edict, and the Ogle Cortina GT could no doubt manage that on its lowered suspension, wide wheels and Dunlop SPs. His car was finished in pale green but, not entirely surprisingly, there were no takers for replicas from coachbuilder Harold Radford at £1500 a throw.

September 1964

A new dished steering wheel is said to be safer in a crash, and seatbelt lugs are now inbuilt.

The mix of Cortina, race champ Moss and design gurus Ogle was certainly a dream – for publicists, any road

September 1964

Along with the general facelift, the Cortina gains the huge advantage of the revolutionary Aeroflow interior through-flow ventilation system.

So what else were you going to buy?

It's amazing to look back to 1963, the first complete year the Cortina was on sale, and discover that there were precious few roomy family cars with 1.2-litre engines. The cheap-and-reasonably-cheerful Cortina was indeed forging a new market segment that had hitherto been ignored.

The Vauxhall Viva and Triumph Herald were cramped by comparison, although attractive cars in their own, feeble-performing way. The Volkswagen Beetle, meanwhile, was a close match for engine size, and its reliability and economy offered superb ownership prospects. But that was tight inside, too. Besides, the engine was at the wrong end.

The hottest rival was the

Morris 1100, and its Austin twin, but these were front-wheel drive cars with weird suspension systems, pathetic boot space and a spooky interior. The Hillman Minx was a viable rear-drive alternative, but that one looked and drove like yesterday's car. The Morris Minor, undoubtedly characterful, was even more aged. Skoda Octavia or Fiat 1300; er, a bit foreign, weren't they?

For the bigger-engined Cortina Super, the obvious alternatives were the Austin Cambridge/Morris Oxford duo or the Hillman Super Minx, all of which cost rather more. The Vauxhall Victor, however, was a credible – if deadly dull – rival, and actually a bit cheaper than a Consul Cortina Super.

June 1965

The bespoke and rather fragile coil-spring suspension on the Lotus-Cortina is changed to cheaper, more robust leaf springs.

Cortina rivals but all near-misses – this page, clockwise from top right: Hillman Minx, Vauxhall Victor FB, Fiat 1300/1500 and Morris 1100; and, opposite, the Volkswagen Beetle

September 1965

A general upgrade sees the column-mounted gearshift option axed, and all Cortinas now come with opening front quarter-light windows.

Would you have promised yourself a Saxon?

The 1969 Ford Capri was billed as 'The car you always promised yourself' but the very first Capri or, more formally, the Ford Consul Capri, was a car customers vowed secretly not to buy.

Slow, over-engineered and dripping with automotive Americanisms like fins, twin headlights and whitewall tyres, the 1961 Capri was a pretty lame attempt at a desirable 'personal' coupe'. It was axed after just three years.

But Ford still tried to conjure up something dashing for family men – and women – who, somehow, could insist they didn't need to be yoked to the tedium of a conventional family saloon. And this was it – the Saxon, circa 1963.

Devoted car spotters will instantly recognise the 'CND' rear lights of the Mk I Cortina, because it was on the much-loved best-seller that the Saxon was heavily based. Even the scallop running from the nose to the neatly abbreviated tail is Cortina-like, although the hardtop is totally new.

As with many 'styling exercises', the Saxon has different proposed styling on each side – you can just see the alternative side window treatment on the other side. The Saxon would have been widely deliberated from all angles by regiments of Ford's marketing experts.

Their reaction, though, was a resounding thumbs-down, so it was to be another six years before the car that Flash Harry drivers longed for finally arrived. It would not, however, be tried out on the road because, convincing though the car looks, it was little more than a static mock-up.

September 1965

A cosmetic rethink of the Super estate livery sees the fake wood décor replaced by two-tone paintwork, new chrome side strips and 'Super' badges.

This one never escaped the design studio, and note how the Saxon has different styling on each side

August 1966

Production of what was shortly to become the Mk I ends. By this time the range encompasses a dozen models, ranging in price from £645 to £1010.

The Ford Cortina Mk II

No matter how complacent its competitors were with their products, Ford was never a company to let grass grow under its feet; and while the original Cortina (thankfully, the 'Consul' bit had been airbrushed from its official title in September 1964) was shifting like choc-ices in a heatwave, its designers were soon charging ahead with work on its successor.

The lid was lifted on the result in October 1966. Ford's naming of the newcomer as the 'Mk II' rendered the old one retrospectively the 'Mk I', but consumers were bombarded with an advertising and marketing blitz under the slogan 'New Cortina Is More Cortina'.

To your dad, Player's No 6 alight in one hand and the Cortina Mk II brochure in the other, the raw data must have sent a wave of alarm through the normally placid Old Man. Was this a new car? After all, the 98in wheelbase and 188in overall length of the old and new Cortinas were identical. It was easy to guess that this was a fairly straightforward re-skin of the old model. The entire floorpan and drivetrain was carried over virtually untouched but the sculpted, vaguely Americanised styling had given way to a boxy, clean, and not a little bland,

European shape. The larger 1498cc engine went unchanged too, although the base engine now featured a five-bearing crankshaft and was uprated to 1298cc to offer 54bhp instead of 48.5bhp.

But once your dad was safely ensconced behind the wheel of a demonstrator at the local Ford agent, the thoroughness of Ford's makeover was obvious. For one thing, the airy cabin was now far roomier in the elbow department thanks to the barrel-profiled, curved door panels and side glass giving a bodywork width increase of 2.4in. The track was

Below: every member of England's 1970 World Cup squad was loaned a white 1600E, but red ones, opposite, were available too, of course

Above: ambulance built for the National Coal Board; opposite: Mk II t-t-tested at −40deg F

broader by a similar amount, making this new Cortina feel even more surefooted, and now even the lowliest version came with standard front disc brakes to best handle the performance from the livelier motors.

Talking of 'basic-ness', this new Cortina was notably more welcoming. Ford's beancounters had sanctioned the fitting of carpets where previously your dad's Hush Puppies and mum's Dr Scholls had had to make do with rubber mats. The slick new dashboard with its padded surround was a vast improvement and, while hardly in Aston Martin DB5 territory, there was notably less bare painted metal than before.

Two- and four-door saloons and a spacious five-door estate were all on offer. Ford positively encouraged its customers to head upmarket by making the Cortina Standard versions available to special order only. For the most stingy private buyer or, most likely, company car manager, such

old-fashioned horrors as a bench front seat and a column-mounted gearlever could still be ordered. Meanwhile, Ford stoked dad-ly aspirations ever further with its GT, 1600E and Lotus editions of the Mk II; they're all lovingly covered in the next few pages, so don't worry.

Little more than a year after the Mk II's launch came a range of brand new engines, popularly known as the 'Kent Crossflow'. These featured crossflow heads with bowl-in-piston combustion chambers, which made them both more efficient and more powerful and responsive. The smaller 1297cc engine now offered a decent 58bhp and its big brother, newly expanded to 1599cc, had 71bhp on tap…and a rasping 88bhp in GT tune.

Little wonder that, in 1967, the Cortina in Mk II form and available in a bewildering 15 versions, became the nation's best-selling single car, with an incredible 14.9% of the total market all to itself; to do this, 165,123 examples had to be delivered to us Brits (with 125,849 more sold elsewhere and including Cortinas now assembled at Ford's Amsterdam plant).

This achievement was probably a first for Ford although, as national sales figures had only been published for individual cars in Britain since 1965, it was impossible to be sure. But for dads nationwide, it was satisfying confirmation that they had indeed made the right choice of family chariot. By 1970, when the last Mk II was built, 1,024,869 had been snapped up.

Even the less overtly sporty versions of the Mk II Cortina (and let's face it, these were the ones most of our paternal figures were bumbling around in, weren't they?) won the immediate respect of many a motoring pundit.

The boffins from *Autocar* magazine got their hands on a 1300 De Luxe two-door in 1966, costing £669, and summed up with: 'Slightly improved performance and much more refinement. Lighter clutch and faultless all-synchromesh gearbox. Fade-free brakes.' They were less enamoured with the seats, which were rather uncomfortable. Testers at the rival *Motor* magazine got stuck into a four-door model, and were altogether more forthright: 'Our overall impression was that the new Cortina is a very sound, sensible car; it is lively, quiet and roomy but some of its controls are not so light and responsive as before.' They were mostly talking about the steering, but they also found the boot to be smaller, fuel consumption higher, and the car likely to pitch about under heavy braking. Still, as *Motor* shrugged: 'What makes it remarkable is the price. Where else can you get so much for £669?'

The same publication found the 1.6-litre crossflow-engined Cortina a tad underwhelming in its 1967 test, finding it harsh at low speeds but with an acceptably long-legged ability at higher cruising speeds on open roads. Then again, Ford was keen to get you into a more expensive GT or 1600E if you were a press-on sort of pater, so perhaps the basic 1600 was made like that on purpose!

But, of course, the typical Cortina was rarely about performance alone, and the estate car versions in particular were trusty and especially capacious because the rear seat back folded down completely flush with the floor, to give exceptionally good cargo room. This was one feature of the Cortina estate highlighted by no less than America's *Road & Track* magazine in 1969… for, surprisingly, the Cortina Mk I and Mk II were quite popular as Ford imports during the 1960s. In a test of 10 imported 'station wagons', it rated the $2208 Cortina as a competent mid-ranger, but recommended it primarily as having the 'best dealer network'. By comparison, the Hillman Hunter estate had the 'smoothest engine', the Datsun 510 was the 'best looking', the Fiat 124 the 'most fun' and the Volkswagen 1600 estate offered the 'highest resale' value. Would those judgements have applied in the UK? Probably. But, then again, your dad probably still went for a Cortina anyway.

Opposite: 70.5 sq ft of flat, empty space; below: dig the Mk II GT's pukka go-faster stripes

The Cortina gave Dagenham its heydays

Every British Ford Cortina started its life at Dagenham, the east London outreach on the marshy, northern bank of the River Thames, where Ford's gigantic factory dominated not just the skyline but every aspect of local life too.

Ford originally set up shop in Britain in Manchester, but identified Dagenham as a much better spot for expansion, because of its deep-water shipping facilities. Edsel Ford, whose dad Henry founded the firm, dug the first sod on 17 May 1929, and the initial vehicle – a Model A truck – rolled off the production line on 1 October 1931. This was soon followed by the Ford Model Y Popular, famously the first British saloon offered at £100.

By the time the first Cortina was built, the 500-acre plant was a wonder of organised labour and private capital: Ford employed 40,000 people at Dagenham which, along with other British factories, turned out 529,127 Ford cars, trucks and tractors that year, 1962. It was such an important industrial edifice that Dagenham's fortunes were often used as a bellwether for the whole British economy.

This picture shows the millionth Cortina for export, a Mk II, being airlifted to its no doubt thrilled purchaser in Belgium in 1970.

Sadly, car manufacture stopped at Dagenham in 2002, although the place is still a major source of diesel engines.

Timeline:
The Ford Cortina Mk II

September 1966

Production cranks into life of
the Cortina Mk II at Dagenham
as the last few of the 1m-plus
Mk Is are being shifted by
Britain's Ford dealer network.

How to create an instant classic for peanuts

Occasionally, a car comes along that catches the public mood perfectly – like the 1967 Ford Cortina 1600E. Its wild success came as much as a surprise to Ford itself as the car delighted British drivers. You hadn't realised you wanted something like this until you saw it.

The 'E' stood for Executive, the inferred target being the new breed of prospering businesspeople getting ahead on their own merits rather than social class or family connections. Ford spotted this emerging demographic and devised this stylish, fast car with an honest heart especially for it.

A £1415 Rover 2000 TC may have been beyond your dad's budget, or entitlement, but at £982 this was just as sexy.

It was a simple exercise involving no new investment. Here was basically a Cortina GT four-door but with the stiffer, lowered suspension of the Lotus-Cortina, and gleaming, wide Rostyle steel wheels setting it off a treat along with several unique paint colours. The seats were replica leather buckets, the carpets thick, the dashboard and door cappings wooden, and the steering wheel aluminium-spoked.

The 1600E was sporty, luxurious and responsive but mechanically predictable. Every Alpha male, dads and sons alike, wanted one. Ford was deluged with orders, selling 60,087, including 2749 rare two-doors for export only, and it became one of the first Cortinas to attain 'classic' status.

September 1966

Both two-door and four-door Cortinas arrive in the showrooms together. There are two four-cylinder engine choices, a new five-bearing 1298cc and the larger, familiar 1498cc, and a choice of De Luxe or Super specification. Prices kick off at £669.

Ford confirms that the Standard version
will be available to special order only;
however, for skinflint buyers, the bench
front seat and column gearchange,
somewhat bafflingly, return as options.

Ford's motor sport mastery went on and on

In the bustling Cortina world of the late 1960s, the new Lotus – now, officially, Ford 'Cortina-Lotus', rather than 'Lotus-Cortina' – struggled for attention as the 1600E hogged the limelight.

The Lotus 1558cc twin-cam engine was upped to 110bhp, but there were no aluminium panels and the car was built on the regular Ford production line. Still, it enjoyed the MK II's wider track and offered servo-assisted brakes. The Lotus's métier was competition. Hence, options included specialised items like a limited-slip differential and oil cooler.

In 1966 and 1967 Bengt Söderström used one, complete with revised rear suspension, to win three world rallies – the Greek Acropolis, the British RAC, and the Swedish – while Ove Anderson also won the Gulf-London rally later in 1967.

In 1967 and 1968, Vic Preston Junior and Peter

Huth took second places in the Safari Rally. And Roger Clark's car was leading the 1968 epic London-Sydney Marathon until his engine failed near the end.

Mk IIs track-raced impressively throughout 1967. Indeed, the Lotus-Cortina was still a pacesetter when Ford introduced the Escort Twin-Cam. It packed the Cortina virtues of speed and strength in a more agile competition package.

The Lotus-Cortina was correspondingly renamed Cortina Twin-Cam in 1968; in this strangely muted form, it lingered on until 1970, when the last of 4032 was built.

September 1966

The Mk II GT is launched too, in two- and four-door saloon iterations. They sport a twin-choke Weber carburettor and a high-level instrument binnacle for press-on drivers.

CORTINA

The five-door estate Cortina Mk II joins the saloons on the tracks at Dagenham.

The Savage – 'a wolf in sheep's clothing'

Did Ford overlook any market opportunity with its Mk II Cortina. Ex-racing driver Jeff Uren thought so. He turned it into an astounding 'Q car' – a high-performance saloon with an unassuming exterior. Most think the term derives from the discreet 'Q boats', WW1 Royal Navy destroyers disguised as merchant ships. Funnily enough, the first known reference to a 'Q car' is in *Motor Sport* magazine in 1963, describing…the Mk I Lotus-Cortina!

Mr Uren installed the 3-litre V6 engine from the Ford Zodiac in his Savage 3000. This compact motor gave a thumping 144bhp, over 50% more oomph than a Cortina GT. Engine mountings, driveline, front discs, radiator and cooling fan were uprated to cope, plus wider wheels and a Powr-Lok rear differential.

There was nothing amateur about this conversion and, while the exterior was deliberately kept indistinguishable from ordinary Cortinas, Uren's Race Proved company could create a sumptuous interior with leather upholstery and a sliding sunroof.

It proved superb to drive, road testers finding it docile around town, fast-accelerating, and an unruffled cruiser. 'The astonishing yet undramatic overtaking performance is a big safety factor', gushed *Car* magazine.

Prices started at £1439 for a two-door, rising to £1576 for an estate. One owner reportedly said: 'I am highly satisfied beyond any expectations, so much so that I have sold my Bentley'. Little wonder Race Proved built 440 Savages between July 1967 and June 1969.

January 1967

In an unusual move, the estate goes on sale first in GT form.

February 1967

Just in case nervous customers thought Ford had lost the plot, Super and De Luxe editions of the estate are released. Prices of these practical cars start at £762.

February 1967

The GT gets close-ratio gears, an advantage later spread to all Cortina variants.

Why go to Butlin's when you could be camping?

Here's a unique Mk II Cortina to gladden the hearts of dads, mums and, of course, us kids who enjoyed the outdoor life. This gleaming white one-off was among the biggest draws at the 1968 London Motor Show, mobbed by Cortina fanatics and camping enthusiasts alike.

Of course, it would have been impossible to accommodate a family of four inside the car for a night's sleep. So the two children got the load bay for their sleeping bags, with the backs of the front seats lifting out and folding flat to make 'ingenious pillow rests'. Ma and Pa could attach the Maréchal 'Family 5/6 lightweight' tent to the back of the car to stay close by.

The kitchen unit was kept in the boot, usable with the tailgate raised or else slid out on its runners to prepare that al fresco fry-up on the Dudley stove. Then the attendant washing up could be tackled in the tiny plastic sink.

The Camping Car also came complete with inflatable mattresses and armchairs, folding dining table and chairs, and space-saving zip-up luggage, all unpacked from the permanent roof rack. It was sponsored by *The Daily Telegraph*, who appointed five designers to plan it and Crayford Auto Development to build it. This company also offered replicas and supplied the individual bits, which could have included the modified 'camping seats' at £39, interior neon strip lights at £14 – even the full set of Harben camping pans, at £7.

Happy days; still, you can probably see why bed-and-breakfasts boomed, can't you?

February 1967

Build of the Mk II Lotus-Cortina starts, at Dagenham this time rather than with Lotus…

March 1967

…and a few weeks later the first Lotus-Cortinas make their much-anticipated appearance on Ford forecourts.

The Daily Telegraph Camping Car

Just how much patience was needed to live with the Telegraph's Cortina camper is hard to gauge from the sun-kissed brochure

A new getaway idea in motoring

Take a Ford Cortina 1600 Estate. Convert it to take everything from a tent to a combined kitchen and vanity unit—and you get the idea of The Daily Telegraph Camping Car. The conversion is surprisingly inexpensive. And you can build up the equipment as you need it. Meanwhile, when the car isn't taking you camping it's a normal family saloon. Five designers were specially invited by The Daily Telegraph Magazine to work on this most exciting project. Margaret Casson, Tom Karen, Vernon Thornton, Robin Bernhard and David Bartlett. Crayford Auto-Development were picked to do the conversion work on the car including Cibié headlights for the Continental night, fog spot lamps, special roof rack and cover, modified suspension, power-brakes and special camping seat modifications.

The extra equipment The Daily Telegraph Camping Car is designed to carry and which you buy separately includes a Marlechal Family Tent, a kitchen unit, sleeping bags, folding tables and chairs, inflatable furniture and special personal luggage including a wardrobe case. The whole of this stows in The Daily Telegraph Camping Car, leaves the rear view clear and still leaves plenty of space for two children to sleep or play while you drive to the site. That's designing for you . . . and the net result is a major advance in holiday making ideas, a real chance for every family to get away, right away, with a minimum of fuss, a maximum of luxury and at an amazingly low cost.

The kitchen unit Slides out on runners and includes a Dudley Stove. It stores food, has a wash bowl and front hinges down to make full length work shelf. It doubles as vanity unit and has legs for separate sitting with wind shields. Folds into a compact unit (see above) for easy storage.

Personal luggage Designed specially by Margaret Casson, stows away easily when you're on the road. Includes wardrobe case, zipped bags, and waterproof cover for four sleeping bags.

Inflatable furniture Folds up and stows handily, inflated by a special engine adaptor. Includes chairs and air mattresses. In addition there is storage for folding table and chairs.

The Car A Ford Cortina 1600 Estate model, converted by Crayford Auto-Development Limited of Westerham, Kent, now sleeps two.

The Equipment Here it is . . . and it all stows neatly and quickly. It leaves the rear window clear when stowed and there's still room for two to sleep or play.

The Tent Fits onto back of car or can be sited separately. Marlechal "Family 3/6" lightweight. It stows in the roof rack.

The back seats fold flat and backs of front seats lift out, turn over and make ingenious pillow rests.

July 1967

The last of the 1498cc engines are manufactured.

August 1967

A new range of 'Kent' engines now equipped with crossflow heads comes on stream, in 1297 and 1599cc sizes. To denote the changeover, the cars now carry 1300 or 1600 badges on the back.

The Cortina keeps Constables comfortable

The very first police 'Panda' car, though not a Cortina, was still a Ford. It was introduced in 1965 by the go-ahead Lancashire Constabulary, which 33 years earlier was the first force to equip its patrol cars with radio communication.

Unlike the bigger 'area' cars as depicted on TV's *Z-Cars*, the Ford Anglia Panda cars weren't meant for chasing criminals. Named for their black- or blue-and-white livery, they were a way to give police constables more speed, weather protection and, of course, the benefit of two-way radio.

However, as *The Daily Mail* has forever bemoaned since, they were the start of bobbies conducting their beats from behind a steering wheel, rather than by flat-footed walking, so Pandas really do have a chequered reputation.

Panda car drivers didn't use sirens, and nor were they trained in defensive driving techniques.

The Mk II Cortina, of course, with its pedestrian and high-performance engine range, was a popular police car in all roles. As a trusty 1300, it saw Panda service nationwide, while as the Lotus-Cortina as shown here on duty in 1969, it provided unexpected speed and handling for high-speed chases and other interventionist manoeuvres. Anyone's dad would want to be the right side of the law if he spotted this in his rear-view mirror…

Perhaps it was no surprise that high-powered Cortinas found favour with the fuzz. You've got to fight fire with fire. After all, Bruce Reynolds, one of the architects of the 'Great Train Robbery' in 1963, was a staunch advocate of souped-up Lotus-Cortinas for both recces and getaways.

August 1967

Every Cortina is now more inviting thanks to dashboards which are all covered in black vinyl, instead of some being bare painted metal. Controls for the Aeroflow ventilation are made more tactile too.

August 1967

Carpets now completely usurp rubber mats across the whole range.

August 1967

Useful detail changes include a centre console clock for the GT, a GT-type remote control gearlever for the Super, while reclining seats are now standardised on all four-doors.

The perfect Cortina for the breezy Dad

Fresh air-addicted fathers had long bemoaned advances in car construction techniques when the first Cortina arrived. This new family car was the usual disappointment. There would be no wind through the (thinning) hair because Ford didn't offer a convertible; far too irksome and expensive to do because an integral-chassis car like the Cortina would have to be redesigned virtually from scratch.

However, the enterprising Crayford Engineering, of Westerham, Kent, spotted a demand for an open tourer, as a bigger alternative to the Triumph Herald convertible. It set about converting the Mk I by sawing the roof off and then artfully strengthening the body with welded steel inserts so it wouldn't collapse after losing its roof's torsional strength.

A few dozen were sold, but Crayford decided to go to town on the Mk II, persuading Ford to give them two blue two-door 1300s even before the new Cortina had been announced. They managed to get one of them converted in just two weeks so it could make its debut simultaneously with the 'whole' car in 1966.

Crayford offered a simple drop-top convertible and also a neater cabriolet, where the folded hood disappeared completely. Not cheap: a convertible conversion on a Lotus-Cortina turned a £1069 tin-top saloon into a £1473 open tourer. Yet they still managed to tempt 400 buyers.

Obviously, in our picture, 'N' denotes the car in question. 'A-M' and 'O' are other Ford-based Crayford custom jobs; even assuming the caption wasn't lost to the mists of time, we don't have the space to describe their myriad upgrades.

September 1967

Ford's masterstroke of Cortina cross-pollination produces the 1600E, mixing a luxurious interior with the sporting features of the GT and the lairy attitude of the Lotus-Cortina.

October 1968

The Lotus-Cortina is renamed
the Twin Cam, as well as gaining
neat touches like a leather-
covered steering wheel and
a centre console clock.

The Cortina jolts Ford's competitors into action

Autumn 1966 brought the first serious attempt to emulate the Cortina's super-successful formula and meet it head-on. The concurrent launch of the Cortina Mk II may have overshadowed it somewhat, but the Hillman Hunter put dads – for the first time in yonks – in a quandary about what they might pick next.

Like the Cortina, the Hunter was a rear-drive, four-cylinder family saloon with pleasing modern styling, MacPherson strut front suspension, and a roomy cabin. It kept pace with the Cortina, not just in its similar size and packaging but also by offering an estate and plenty of choice in Hillman Minx, Singer Gazelle and Humber Sceptre editions. For a time, it was the most convincing alternative on offer. There was even a little machismo, in the Hunter GT.

Elsewhere, Fiat's Lada-type 124 and 125 saloons were spirited Cortina baiters, while some were tempted by Vauxhall's slightly smaller Viva or slightly larger Victor instead of the Ford.

During the late 1960s, the first Japanese imports began, and the Toyota Corona and Datsun 1600 were the first challengers to the Cortina's rule from the Far East. There was lukewarm opposition from France's Simca 1301, although the Renault 16 offered something the Cortina lacked – a hatchback.

Two niche cars lured some buyers of more specialised Cortinas. The front-wheel drive Triumph 1300 was an interesting and luxurious substitute, and a BMW 1602 made a feisty, if expensive, change from a 1600E.

October 1968

A new black-painted radiator grille distinguishes all Cortinas, along with new 'FORD' badging front and rear. A remote control gearchange is standardised across all models too.

The Mk II met a close match in the Hillman Hunter (bottom right) and Fiat 124 (left); BMW's '02' series (bottom left) lured away some well-off punters, and the hatchback Renault 16 (below) was a mighty versatile family alternative

October 1968

Reclining seats become an optional feature on two-door models. They are improved support-wise across the whole range too.

The Cortina Mk II shapes the motorway age

The Ford Cortina and Britain's motorway network: chicken and egg? Well, it's difficult to know which one was the 'driver' of the other.

True, the first stretch of motorway arrived four years before Ford's much-loved saloon. It was the Preston By-pass (now part of the M6), which opened on 5 December 1958, although it was only 8.2 miles long. But the main event came a year later, on 2 November 1959, when the M1 opened between Watford and Rugby.

By the time the Cortina Mk II was into its stride, it had been extended down to London and up to Leeds.

The average British car of 1958/9 was not really up to the sustained high speeds that motorway driving demanded, but in this role the lightweight, rev-happy, unstressed Cortina excelled. So, as sales of Cortinas rocketed, demand for further motorways to drive them on also snowballed, and the whole of Britain was opened up as never before. Whether it was away on business or hitching up the caravan for long-distance driving holidays, your dad could now set out in his Mk II confident he wouldn't spend interminable hours – one eye on the temperature gauge – sitting in traffic jams through narrow country towns.

Motorways had no speed restrictions at all until a 70mph upper limit was introduced in November 1965 as a four-week experiment. On 22 December it became permanent; just days later, Labour's Barbara Castle became the first woman transport minister and had to face the flak from a fuming motoring press, the AA, and the Tories. But the limit has stuck ever since.

October 1968

The GT receives a mild upgrade, with a revised centre console, floor-mounted handbrake, and the instruments previously mounted in a separate binnacle now re-housed within the facia. Rear seats are now moulded bucket-style too.

AVX 118G

October 1968

Cortinas gain an interior bonnet release mechanism, which makes the car harder to steal.

LUF 698F

"It's a full-time job. Now behave yourself."

"I don't send 'em solicitors' letters. I apply a bit of pressure." These menacing words, from Michael Caine, typified the crackling script of brooding, 1971 British thriller *Get Carter*.

Caine, as urbane London villain Jack Carter, travels to his home town of Newcastle, ostensibly to arrange his brother's funeral – but, actually, to find out who killed him and exact his own brutal, unflinching revenge.

Refusing to accept the police report of suicide, Carter seeks out his brother's friends and acquaintances, but finds a wall of stony silence from the local underworld. "You're a big man, but you're in bad shape", he says to one. "With me it's a full-time job. Now behave yourself".

Operating on a hunch, he tails sleazy chauffeur Eric (Ian Hendry) to local crime lord Kinnear's (John Osbourne) home. Surprisingly, Carter's welcomed in, but is warned to return to London. Only then does he set out on a path of vengeance against those implicated in his brother's death. For this dark Geordie odyssey, Carter rents a two-door Mk II Cortina Super. This silver Cortina features extensive memorably bashing the front passenger door clean off a pristine Mk2 Jaguar as he makes a hasty escape and the film heads towards its downcast ending.

It's probably the most vivid Mk II moment on celluloid although, by bizarre contrast, you'll also find one in Hollywood production *Alligator* (1980) where the overgrown reptile, having become enormous in the New York sewers, attempts to eat the unsuspecting Cortina…

October 1968

A better interior aura is now assured on all Cortinas as the steering column, steering wheel and vents are all coordinated with the upholstery. Nice.

CAINE is CARTER

MGM-EMI PRESENTS
A MICHAEL KLINGER PRODUCTION
MICHAEL CAINE
in
GET CARTER x

Co-starring
IAN HENDRY · JOHN OSBORNE
and **BRITT EKLAND**

Screenplay **Mike Hodges**
Based on the novel "JACK'S RETURN HOME" **Ted Lewis**
Produced by **Michael Klinger**
Directed by **Mike Hodges**
Metrocolor · Released by MGM-EMI

July 1970

The final Mk II Cortinas in the 14-strong model range are built.

The Ford Cortina Mk III

Europe's a big place, but not that big, and in the end it simply had to happen: British and German design teams were merged to turn the third-generation Cortina (alongside its Taunus equivalent) into a proper Euro-Ford. And, internal arguments and wrangling notwithstanding, they did a superb job.

Actually, it wasn't the first time Dagenham and Cologne had co-operated. The changing face of Europe had dictated that, no matter what your dad might have joshed about French personal hygiene or the average German's inability to get a punchline.

Ford's quandary had been the troublesome split between those European countries within the Common Market and those outside it; these represented markets of 200m and 100m consumers respectively, and Britain was in the smaller group. Despite the fact that Ford was heading for dominance of the British market, the Common Market countries with their rapidly melting trade tariffs offered even juicier prospects. And, throughout the 1960s, it was far from obvious that Britain would ever cross the divide.

Still, it was simply crackers for Ford to be creating parallel ranges of near-identical cars in Europe. Heads began to be knocked together by the bosses in Detroit. They forced British and German designers and engineers to jointly-develop a new van, and so the 1965 Transit became the first truly

European Ford vehicle. Next, Ford Germany was obliged to accept the 1967 Escort, wholly created in Britain to replace the Anglia, as its own new small car. Ha!

But also in that year, Ford of Europe was finally created to bring all the continent's activities under one umbrella. Headquartered in Essex but with operations in Britain, Belgium and Germany, the new single entity began to tidy up its messy organisation. The first wholly European car was the 1969 Capri. And the second was the all-new Cortina, for which eight, 4in-thick volumes of *European General*

Below: this 1600XL did 45,077 UK miles on the same tyres in a 1970s publicity stunt

Product Acceptance data was collated to get the car spot-on; 82 prototypes were tested to destruction; and 300 engines were tested in Capris that covered up to 40,000 miles each. It was the modern equivalent of the old *Red Book* that underpinned the first Cortina. The economies of scale must have made the company's accountants positively gurgle with delight.

So there's the background; what about the machine itself, sitting there all gleaming and new in October 1970?

Whereas the switch from Mk I to Mk II Cortina had amounted to a comprehensive restyling, this time the Mk III was a totally new structure, in which the only carry-over elements were the basically unaltered 1.3- and 1.6-litre engines

Mk IIIs undergoing rigorous roll-over (below) and suspension (opposite) testing

The overall 168in length was actually the same as the Mk II's, but you'd never have guessed it thanks to a 3.5in longer wheelbase, a 2.1in width increase, a 3.5in wider front track and a huge 5in wider rear track. Amusingly, to sell within the right tax bracket in Japan, Cortina body shells had to be clamped and squeezed in a special jig in Dagenham to make them compliantly narrow!

The impression that this was a wholly bigger car was emphasised by lowering the roof height by 2.7in. Together with the lower bonnet line made possible by the compactness of all the engines on offer, the new Cortina looked far more ground-hugging and purposeful, yet it was all a clever illusion.

John Fallis, one of the key designers of the car's shape, said at the time: "Today's environment demands crisp sharp styling. There is a very big glass area with clean, sharp corners to the screens and windows. In purely motoring terms, the trend is towards features associated with high-performance cars".

The most distinctive styling feature, however, was the undulating contour of the wingline, often referred to as the 'Coke bottle' shape. Mr Fallis called this a "hop-up" when he was justifying it: "The raked style of the Cortina's rear screen and bootlid joins nicely with a hop-up feature. It ties in well with the overall movement theme. So does the crease line two thirds of the way down the door, which is continued over the wheelarch to produce a flared look."

So the Cortina was flaring out like the bottom of your dad's suit trousers, eh? Yes, but Mr Fallis had more.

This Cortina, and its roof-mounted contraption, was used in 1971 to track drivers' overtaking manoeuvres

"This emphasis on side sculpturing brings out the best in body colour. It shows off paint – particularly metallic paint – to great effect. You can see the tremendous secondary colour, the sheen, that comes in the car's form when you have shape". And the groovy new metallics on offer included Tawny (a burnt gold), Garnet (a rich red) and Sapphire (a very bright blue).

Which was all very slick, but your pop was possibly more impressed by the boot lid that now opened down to bumper level with the spare wheel under the boot floor – fantastically useful for trips to the tip. The pointed front wing tips gave a new precision to the art of parking and the fuel filler was now concealed behind a metal flap, but opening quarter-lights – much loved by all dads – were sacrificed in the name of super-soaraway seventies sleekness.

Underneath, rack-and-pinion steering was a vast improvement, while new front suspension (coil springs were now fitted all round), supported by upper and lower wishbones, was packaged in a front subframe with the steering and the front of the engine, all the better to contribute to the lower frontal area that characterised this new car. All 1.6- and 2.0-litre cars came with a front anti-roll bar too.

What with dads still prone to driving home from a session at The Red Lion – no matter what Jimmy Savile implored – there was also a collapsible steering column, plus dual-circuit brakes. Sleeping off the effects of too much Toby bitter first was a better idea, made more inviting by reclining seats even on boggo Cortinas

Her mother, presumably, was reassured when he picked her up in a sensible L two-door

The Mk III enjoyed a storming start to sales and, although it was destined to rarely see any serious motor sport action, it was endorsed by the likes of Jackie Stewart ("If a driver is sitting comfortably, there's a good chance he'll drive more safely. The new Cortina seats are outstanding") and Jochen Rindt ("It is so full of style and yet it is loaded with passenger and luggage space"). Prices were higher at the start, ranging from £914 to £1338, but that put no brake on demand. After six years on sale, exactly 1,126,559 were sold – 967,488 saloons and 154,216 estates. A seemingly constantly changing range mix, Britain's deep trust of the Cortina brand, and cruddy competition from Vauxhall and British Leyland propelled the Mk3 Cortina to the top of the sales charts in 1972, where it was to remain the champion for three full years.

The inside story of the Ford Cortina Mk III

Never been inside a Mk III Cortina? The 1970-era cabin seems absurdly low-slung for a family saloon. But that's the effect Ford wanted; it had trained the Cortina up as a motor sport champ – now that brand image needed to rub off on Mr Average.

Of course, multi-purpose vehicles (MPVs) and child seats did not exist then. Your toddlers just frolicked, unbelted, on your Cortina's slippery rear bench, or played on the floor. Still, manoeuvring carrycots into the back of a Mk III was agonising for middle-aged lower backs.

In a Mk III, all the instruments were flamboyantly 'recessed' into a dashboard sloping away dramatically from the driver. Even the ignition slot and choke were deeply 'recessed' in the steering column, for Pete's sake.

The odour of mixed plastics was powerful. There was the hard, shiny black stuff on steering wheel, console, dashboard top, gearknob and handbrake. And then there were the seats. Ford's 'Interior Trim Laboratory' wanted to overturn the British love of leather-look vinyl. While this ghastly stuff was indeed standard on all Cortinas, Ford concocted its own optional 'cloth' upholstery.

Okay, it was really ICI's Bri-Nylon woven by Jersey-Kapwood Ltd so that it stretched without bagging, and coated so biro could be cleaned off with meths, and spilt salad cream wouldn't stain (no, really – they tested it). But it was a start.

The interiors of Mk III-era Cortinas were always trashy, that's for sure. Still, for 1970s punters, they were a major relief after the intimidating, barren minimalism found in British Leyland's 1300 and 1800 cars.

Timeline:
The Ford Cortina Mk III

October 1970

The all-new Cortina Mk III makes its debut in a hugely ambitious range right from the start – there are 32 different versions on offer as two-door saloon, four-door saloon and five-door estate. Prices begin at £914, rising to £1338 for a 2000 GXL.

How the Cortina and Taunus were the same

The Mk III Cortina was meant to be a Euro-Ford, pure and simple, ending the pointless duplication that characterised earlier parallel British and German efforts. But then the marketing folk in Dagenham and Cologne dug their heels in and insisted their respective customer pools were subtly different.

That's why, although the Cortina III and Taunus TC (aha! That stood for Taunus Cortina!) were largely the self-same car, they look a tiny bit different. The most obvious change is to the beltline, which undulates sexily on the Cortina and is straighter and more severe on the Taunus. Grilles, bonnets and boots all varied slightly too.

The two ranges diverged further. The Taunus 1.6 GT used Ford Germany's overhead-camshaft engine, the Cortina 1.6 GT used the Pinto unit. The Pinto 2-litre was the top UK engine while the ultimate German cars came with a locally-made V6. And – the biggest difference of all – there was an autobahn-munching Taunus fastback coupé, but no Cortina equivalent.

At the dual launch in 1970, there were 34 Taunus models versus 29 Cortinas; then again, you could get 14 paint colours on a Cortina but only 11 on a Taunus. So, nurr.

Some European markets saw both types of Ford competing, but fathers – and, indeed, *Vater* – disposed to anxiety could relax. No matter where they drove in Europe, Ford dealers were obliged to offer identical levels of service for all Cortina IIIs and Taunus TCs.

October 1970

The new line up includes four basic four-cylinder engines: the familiar overhead-valve 'Kent' units in 1287cc and 1599cc sizes (available in low- and high-compression tune), and 1593cc and 1993cc overhead-camshaft 'Pinto' motors.

October 1970

Instead of the old Standard/De Luxe/Super specification range strategy, the new Cortina offers a 'Custom Plan' system, whereby buyers can order their cars with the engine they want plus appointments no a new sliding scale of luxury which starts at Base and works its way up through L, XL and GT to GXL.

Cortina estates didn't shift expectations

The Cortina estate should have topped off many dads' lists for both dependability and usefulness. Yet the statistics prove that, with 154,216 estate cars sold between 1970 and 1976, only about 15% of buyers actually went for the five-door, cargo-happy option.

With out-of-town shopping in its infancy in Britain, and mostly confined to garden centres and a few DIY superstores, perhaps a large estate car then wasn't as handy as your father would find it now. After all, with no Ikea yet open in the UK, flat-pack furniture was rare; if you bought a new sideboard, chances are a Maples van delivered it ready-built.

Still, for holidays, weekly shops and Sunday morning runs to the council tip, the Mk III estate was supreme. Once again, with rear seats folding

completely flat and the spare wheel beneath the boot floor, the load bay was unencumbered. It was the roomiest Cortina estate ever: 33.2cu ft of luggage space with the rear seat up and, when folded, this nearly doubled to 63.8cu ft.

Regretfully, the strangely exciting GT derivative was no more, the estate initially coming in merely Standard, L and XL forms (a 2000E was added much later). The Standard always had rubber mats lining the luggage compartment but the L and XL generally came with a nice bit of carpet back there.

April 1972

A much improved automatic transmission, the C2, is offered on certain models.

In an effort to simplify the huge Cortina range for both overwhelmed dealers and customers, the two-door GXL option is culled.

Good, clean, politically-incorrect family fun

How entirely fitting that the Ford Cortina Mk III should be a regular feature of *Bless This House*, one of the most consistently popular sit-coms on ITV throughout the whole of the car's time on Ford forecourts.

For *Bless This House* was the ongoing comic saga of weary dad Sid Abbott, the Putney stationery salesman constantly perplexed by his dippy son and flirty daughter, and under the permanent thumb of wife Jean. 'Meet Sid', went the publicity, 'the head of the household (that's what he thinks!)'. All Sid desires is his pipe, a few pints, barmaids' legs to ogle, and a Chelsea win. From this humdrum pretext, the gags and embarrassment flowed.

Sid, played to sly perfection by the great Sid James, drives a Mk III two-door throughout the show's 65 episodes from 1971–6. It's never parked in the garage, which doubles as son Mike's art studio.

In the spin-off *Bless...* movie, the scenario is revisited but Sid now drives a groovy yellow Cortina III estate.

New comic possibilities were provided by toffee-nosed neighbour Ronald Baines, portrayed by Terry Scott, particularly when Sid's Cortina smacks into Baines's Vauxhall Viscount and the two indignant suburbanites come to blows. How we chortled when a removal driver says: "Has his steering gone?", and Baines replies: "I don't know whether it's his steering, or him!"

Bless This House can now be enjoyed, if that's the right word, again on DVD.

September 1973

The Cortina range is comprehensively refreshed, with all cars receiving a new grille design and a better quality, less tacky facia.

September 1973

Subtle but welcome revisions to gearing, now featuring closer ratios, and suspension make all Cortinas better to drive.

September 1973

The XL gains rectangular headlamps and a distinctive body coachline.

AOO 956M

Two types of GT for the 'gran turismo' chap

One of the odder aspects of the MK III was that, despite its racier styling and laid-back driving position, it brought the overtly performance-orientated Cortina era to an end.

There was no Lotus-reworked edition to get pulses racing. The GT specification was now, in its most powerful edition, a definite case of style over content. The 1993cc 98bhp Pinto engine was identical to that offered in basic L, comfortable XL, and opulent GXL configurations. The 2-litre GT nonetheless maintained its go-faster image with a coachline, matt black trim, 'sports road wheels', radial tyres and a smattering of superfluous instruments like an oil pressure gauge. The most obviously sporty feature was the rally-type, high-back front seats in sticky black vinyl that, said Ford, 'look good enough for a jet liner cockpit'. Hmm; Albanian Airways, maybe.

Lower down the Cortina pecking order was the main focus of GT fascination for your pops. The 1593cc overhead-camshaft Pinto unit for the GT was distinct from the overhead-valve Kent offered for other 1.6-litre trim levels. Its extra 10bhp reduced the 0–60mph time from a leaden 14.9sec to a spritely 11.9. Top speed leapt from 91 to 101mph yet – as dads were relieved to discover – GT fuel consumption dropped just 2mpg from 30 to 32. Phew!

September 1973

The slick 2000E model is announced as a range-topper, aiming to recapture the past glory of the Mk II 1600E, with a wood dashboard, luxurious upholstery and trim, and a vinyl roof as standard. It replaces the GXL.

September 1973

The 1.6-litre Kent engine is dropped, its place taken in the range by wider use of the 1.6-litre Pinto power pack.

Ford offered the Cortina pick-me-up

Here's one Cortina Mk III that there's virtually no chance of coming across in Britain.

That's because this highly unusual commercial vehicle model was assembled and sold exclusively on the South African market. Could it have stood a chance on Britain's tradesmen's market? It seems more than likely. After all, when this picture was taken outside Ford's Port Elizabeth plant in South Africa in 1971, Mazda's broadly similar B1600 '1-ton' pick-up and Toyota's Hi-Lux were picking up sales worldwide. They would shortly be enjoying strong sales in the UK, too…with not a hint of competition from Ford.

The weird thing is, the chassis-cab shown here, with its sturdy bodywork platform and rugged leaf springs, did actually originate in Dagenham like all other members of the Cortina family. Exactly 4855

of them, in kit form, set sail south to the Cape for local assembly in the Ford plant there and fitment of a locally-made 'bakkie' – the slang word for pick-up – body. They would have travelled alongside kits for thousands more Cortina saloons due to be bolted together in the same fashion.

It may not have been an elegant piece of design. That rear cab panel, for instance, has all the finesse of the backside of a typical washing machine. But, hey, at least they found somewhere to squeeze the spare wheel…

The fact is, with the massively popular Transit in its product arsenal, Ford probably saw little need to try and persuade British business that a Cortina pick-up made sense. And it would never have been much of an image-booster for the Cortina itself, now, would it?

September 1974

A new pinnacle of station wagon luxury is offered as a 2000E estate joins the line-up.

The New Ford Cortina 2000E Estate Car.

The GT option remained
the sportiest Cortina
on offer, albeit with
untuned engines.

The jewel in my crown: the Ford Cortina 2000E

The Mk III 2000E will always float the Cortina boat for me, because this is the one my dad had.

Not, I hasten to add, as a new car, or even as a glittering reward for his achievements on the greasy pole (his firm offered no company car perk). No, we got our 2000E from a used car lot near Grimsby in 1978 complete with bunting and the chirpy gaffer in his sheepskin coat and gold sovereign ring.

Of all the many saloons on his windswept premises, the three-year old 2000E was the one I cajoled Dad to get. It was the tastiest car there, after all, in its metallic silver-blue paintwork, black vinyl roof with chrome 'E' emblems, and fake Minilite wheels.

Inside, it was limousine-like with its velvety seats, thick carpets, tinted glass, and something we'd never had before – a push-button AM/LW radio.

For a month or two, and aged 13, I'd gaze lovingly at our 2000E whenever possible. I'd engineer lifts for schoolfriends, to impress them. My father, though, did not cherish the car. He simply thrashed it, daily. The paint faded; the wooden door cappings blistered and cracked; the whole interior soon reeked of Silk Cut; and the car rusted from the inside out, until the aerial in the front wing fell out and the push-button radio was rendered useless.

In 1982, he traded this careworn jalopy in for a Chrysler Avenger. By then everyone, and everything, had moved on. But I'll always love the 2000E.

October 1975

Ford launches its 'Value for Money' equipment package, with a host of subtle enhancements to the specifications of all Cortinas, while keeping a lid on pricing in the face of rampant inflation.

October 1975

The 2000E is made even more opulent with the addition of front seat headrests at no extra charge.

A *new meaning* to 'metallic copper'

The car chases in *The Sweeney*, first shown in 1975, are some of the finest in TV history, shot like the rest of this ground-breaking police drama on London's mean streets. Dads ensured their younger children were tucked up in bed well before the compelling but gritty and ripe goings-on of London's Flying Squad began at 9pm.

It starred the legendary John Thaw and Dennis Waterman, later of Inspector Morse and Minder fame respectively, as detective inspector Regan and his sergeant Carter. It's synonymous with the tyre-squealing exploits of a certain brown Ford Consul GT. However, the duo used a Mk III Cortina 2-litre GT back-up car just as frequently – driven just as sensationally, too.

The BBC sought to recapture the spirit of *The Sweeney* for *Life On Mars* in 2006, in which John Simm is Sam Tyler, a Manchester detective whose comatose state somehow transports him back to 1973. A Mk III Cortina is waiting there to assist, driven by retro-hardcase DCI Gene Hunt, played by Philip Glenister.

"It was very difficult to handle without power steering", Glenister said afterwards. "I was rather shocked by it. It was a rustbucket really. It was great fun, quite a flash motor for the time."

The Cortina's appearance, though, sparked nerdy controversy when it was noticed the MkIII 2000E featured inexplicably sported GXL front grille and MkIV Cortina dashboard.

October 1975

Base Cortinas gain cloth seats, carpets, hazard warning flashers, a heated rear window and a cigar lighter at no extra cost. But most shiny trim is replaced by matt black on grille, sills and window surrounds.

October 1975

All Cortinas, with the
exception of the Base model,
now come with rectangular
halogen headlamps.

Now look here, sunshine: this Cortina's for you

This sultry little number, photographed in 1971 by Bristol Street Motors' advertising department with the help of models Silk, Erica and Rosie, is the Crayford Sunshine Cortina. You can't help thinking that the decidedly hazy style of the brochure tries hard to compensate for one missing ingredient: not a ray of sunshine is evident anywhere.

What it does do, though, is throw some light on this semi-official Cortina convertible, which was now sold exclusively by Bristol Street Motors at its various big city outlets, with the tin-snipping work performed, as before, by Crayford down in the wilds of Kent.

The Crayford boys took a different tack this time, skinning

off the roof panel and rear window but retaining the upper door and rear window frames to bestow the car with as much integral strength as possible. This cabriolet-type hood design allowed for the whole roof to be peeled back, or else just the front portion in lieu of a wide canvas sunroof.

You may well wonder why anyone would have shelled out hard-earned cash for such a conversion job. The answer is simple: if you wanted an affordable four-seater convertible for the family, then the only choices were the last of the Triumph Heralds, the VW Beetle or, for rather more dosh, a BMW 1600. And not one of those could, really, match a Cortina for, well, normalness.

October 1975

The Cortina GT trim level is lifted by inertia-reel seatbelts, clock, wooden facia and a driver's door mirror. Low profile tyres give the handling a lift.

crayford sunshine cortina

>>>

October 1975

Cortina L and XL estates get rear wash/wipe as standard, a real boon on Britain's windy, drizzly main roads.

The Cortina alternatives were still a motley bunch

The Mk III Cortina, almost uncannily, continued to provide what an overwhelming number of British drivers craved. The size was ideal and the packages of options available suited everyone. Yet despite this successful formula now entering its third generation, direct rivals were still amazingly few.

As the early 1970s dawned, the Hillman Hunter sailed on but wasn't updated, although the more compact Avenger undoubtedly had appeal to some potential Cortina owners. The enlarged Vauxhall Victor, meanwhile, became more of a Granada competitor.

From British Leyland, both the five-door Austin Maxi and the Triumph 1300/1500 had differing merits as alternatives. But the big news was the Morris Marina, one car that really had been modelled along Cortina lines. Throughout the 1970s, the wide Marina range put up a sterling fight in spite of always being an inferior product, and over 1m were sold.

A flotilla of Japanese imports, boasting value and reliability, had varying impacts on the Cortina's rule. Nissan made the biggest inroads with its 1971 Bluebird, the 1972 Toyota Corona was rather less popular, while the 1974 Mitsubishi Colt Galant barely registered.

Gnawing away at the Cortina from the sidelines was Europe's finest, including the Renault 12 and first Volkswagen Passat. By 1975, the Fiat Mirafiori joined them. Contrast that year was provided by the new Chrysler Alpine, never much of a Cortina threat, and the first Vauxhall Cavalier…which did, in fact, eventually mean real business.

February 1976

A new, stripped-out Economy version of the Cortina 1300 goes on sale to keep sales of the cars buoyant through the global fuel crisis. It's not very popular.

British Leyland's Maxi (left) and Marina (below) were chasing Cortina buyers; the Renault 12 (below, left, leapfrogging a Renault 8) was competent; Mk III shows suspicious similarities to Vauxhall Victor FD (below, right)

August 1976

Production of the Mk III ends in readiness for its Cortina replacement.

The Ford Cortina Mk IV

The Ford Cortina was, by 1976, nothing short of a British institution, the default choice for fathers across the land, and pretty much any other buyer who valued robustness, mechanical simplicity, comfort and cheap running costs. In its voluptuous Mk III guise, moreover, the Cortina had melded American styling themes with '70s fashions.

By 1976, the country was hungry for an update. The Mk III had turned from trendy to tacky in the looks department, especially beside the crisp European modernity of pacesetting cars such as the Volkswagen Golf and Renault 5.

After 14 years, though, the momentum of the Ford hit machine seemed to have swung eastwards to Germany. In late spring 1976, a new Taunus range was announced while the Mk III Cortina remained in situ. But when the Cortina Mk IV was finally unveiled in September that year as a 1977 car, the result was a mild shock: finally, you could look from Taunus to Cortina and back to Taunus again and not tell the difference. They were perfect doppelgangers, and so the days of the distinctively British Cortina were finally over, but so was the obvious futility of creating two differing cars.

Still, never mind: this new Cortina possessed a neat, angular, handsome shape. It was very much in the contemporary German idiom, which was no surprise since it was a German who styled it. Uwe Bahnsen had joined Ford Germany as a young designer in the 1950s, and played a major part in the stylish 1960 Taunus 17M – which, you will no doubt love to know, was the very first car in the world with a 'styled' headlight resembling a TV screen. By 1976, he was in charge of all styling at Ford of Europe, and therefore the new Cortina was his direct responsibility.

Below: the Cortina Mk IV saloon and estate prominent in Britain's 1979 Ford range

Cortina Ghia
Luxury in a car that's built to last

The Age of Elegance comes back to beautiful life in the new Cortina Ghia.

The famous engineering skill of Ford blended with the superbly tasteful design flair of the Italian Ghia also make this one of the most practical and luxurious cars in Europe.

Take the coachwork, with the elegant vinyl roof, the smart black vinyl window pillars, the window surrounds with combined black and bright window mouldings. All the window glass is tinted for extra safety and to keep the interior cooler. A remote control door-mounted mirror makes rear-view visibility easier and safer, too. The wide low-slung bodyside moulding is unique to Ghia. It all says luxury. And the Ghia badging is like having your own exclusive coat of arms. Power and comfortable ride are also part of the Cortina Ghia luxury. It has a litre engine with a twin venturi carburettor, gas shock absorbers, 165 SR 13 low profile tyres.

It's a beautiful way to travel.

Taken from Mk IV brochures, these images highlight the new Ghia and S derivatives

Still, once he was out of his *Dad's Army* mindset, the man of your house was no doubt chuffed with Herr Bahnsen's efforts. The new Cortina was chunky on the outside. The bonnet line had been lowered once again after extensive wind tunnel tests to keep the front of the car better anchored to the road in side winds, while a modest steel airdam below the front bumper bolstered high speed stability.

And, once seated in the driving seat, your dad would have found a vastly improved interior with a tidier dashboard and a general design clean-up to rid the car of the late 1960s American overtones so endemic of the Mk III. Visibility was improved, with 15% more glass over the Mk III, while minimum standard equipment now befitted a car of the late 1970s.

Every Cortina, no matter how lowly, had carpets, a cigar (note: emphatically not cigarette!) lighter, driver's door mirror, hazard warning lights, and servo-assisted front disc brakes. Nevertheless, the pecking order was still rigidly observed down to the smallest detail. No 'plastic trinket tray' until you got up to L level, though; no radio until you got up to GL level; and no tinted glass unless you bought a Ghia! But a factory-fitted sliding steel sunroof was a first on a Cortina, available as an option on any of the two- and four-door saloons or five-door estate.

The interior ventilation system was vastly better. Ford was mighty proud of the fact that, bowling along at 70mph, all the air inside it was flushed out and replaced every 18 seconds. A blunt statistic, but invaluable for any dad in a nylon shirt commuting on a hot day, while sucking away on a Manikin.

It added up to a tempting package at any trim or engine level. And yet the Mk IV was entirely a Mk III under its smart new clothes, the mechanical underpinnings being carried over wholesale. No

wonder the latest Cortina, after its initial splash, rapidly came to be considered old fashioned, despite the fact that close attention to rubber bushes in the driveline and suspension had made it quieter and smoother.

The increasingly dated rear-drive layout, though, still inspired enormous confidence among buyers, and the engine range that spanned 1.3-litre economy to 2.3-litre V6 purring power offered something for everyone. The only traditional Cortina element that seemed to be lacking was a model with a real enthusiastic driver appeal. To partly compensate, there was the twin-carburettor Cortina S, which shared its engine with the mainstream GL while offering such go-faster goodies as styled sports wheels (but no alloys), matt black window surrounds and a pair of halogen spotlamps. Its only truly sporty attribute was stiffened-up suspension for slightly tauter cornering.

The Mk IV also sired the biggest-engined

Cortina of all time, a standard four-door saloon with a beefy 4.1-litre straight-six tightly packed under its bonnet. It was a special model assembled in Australia solely for local consumption. Likewise, there was a 3-litre V6 model built and sold only in South Africa.

In the face of competitors offering hatchbacks, fuel-injection and front-wheel drive, the Cortina remained almost bewilderingly popular. At times in the late 1970s, it accounted for one in every seven new cars sold in the UK, and remained at the pinnacle of the sales chart right through to 1980, when the car entered its final phase. Regular outings in blokey detective series *The Professionals*, which was far too violent for children to be allowed to stay up for, only boosted its image as the car that all real men really ought to drive.

Opposite; GL was Cortina acme for most; upholstery, below, could be hideous, but estate was always handy

A Cortina of which Ford seemed ashamed

Rather like an ostracised relative, there was one member of the shiny new Mk IV Cortina family whom we, ahem, didn't like to talk about – a Cortina that was rarely glimpsed and virtually never commented upon.

This outcast was the two-door.

The very first Cortina Mk I to arrive in showrooms had been a two-door saloon. It was the bedrock upon which the car's entire stellar sales career had been based. Such a format, with its tip-forward front seats allowing access to a rear seat that was never cramped or second-rate, had been robustly marketed right up to the very last Mk IIIs.

Yet in all the brochures and advertising for the new Mk IV, few photographs of the two-door were shown at all. Indeed, if your dad combed the small print, he'd have discovered that the two-door –

which, with two small children, made good sense despite the fitment of childproof locks on four-doors – could be ordered only as a 1300 Base or 1300L. This meant the only engine was the weedy 1298cc Kent that could furnish a feeble 82mph top speed and a chronic 0–60mph time of 19.4sec.

Makes you wonder why Ford bothered at all… and yet, right up until the bitter end when the Cortina 80 was nearing the axe in 1982, a 1300 and a 1300L two-door were still on offer.

Timeline:
The Ford Cortina Mk IV

A totally updated Cortina range, the Mk IV offers a vast choice from the off. Just as before, the engine range spans from a 50bhp 1297cc to a 98bhp 1993cc. But destined to be the most popular is the 1593cc engine, initially giving a fairly meek 59bhp.

The vinyl countdown to the new Cortina

The Mk IV subtly changed Ford's strategy for the Cortina. The 'blue oval's sporting image was now dominated by Escort and Capri, so from 1976 the Cortina would be pushed further into luxury territory. For dads with greying temples, emergent love handles, and a general interest in peace and quiet, this was fine. Energetic 20-something fathers may not have been so impressed.

So, while the only vaguely sporting Cortina was now the S, with its halogen spotlights and slightly stiffer suspension, the Ghia livery made its Cortina debut. This Italian coachbuilding name, founded by Giacinto Ghia as a bespoke body shop in 1919, was world-famous for styling by the time Ford bought it in 1973. With a cavalier attitude to its heritage, though, Ford axed coachbuilding and 'Ghia' was soon slapped on luxury editions of the Granada and Mustang II.

For the Cortina Mk IV, this meant no less then crushed velour upholstery, shagpile carpet and that most essential of 1970s upmarket trademarks: a vinyl roof in tan or black. Bellissima, eh!

And to give the new 'ultimate' Cortina the hushed refinement it demanded, a German-built 2296cc V6 engine – borrowed from the Granada – was offered from late '77. Its 108bhp of pulling power, added torque, and relatively silken manners did its best to drag the humble Cortina into junior Merc territory.

It was all a long, long way from the Lotus-Cortina.

September 1976

No more GTs in the Cortina range: its place is taken by the S, which offers no more power than a GL but has stiffer suspension, black window surrounds and a pair of halogen spotlamps.

Nor does the 'E' theme of the 2000E continue. The most luxurious model in the Cortina line-up now adopts the Ghia livery familiar from the Capri and Granada.

The great British estate rolls on regardless

Ford sales figures for the Cortina Mk IV/80 don't specify how many of the cars sold were estates, but it's probable that the figure isn't more than 20%.

These square-backed, van-like workhorses still found a ready market, and large family hatchbacks from other marques, such as the Chrysler Alpine, barely stole any practically-minded fathers away from the Cortina clan. Stick with what you know, dad reckoned, and you can't go wrong.

The Mk IV Cortina estate range was certainly comprehensive. The gutless 1300 engine wasn't available but the 1.6- and 2.0-litre Pinto motors gave adequate and punchy performances respectively, whether in Base, L, GL or Ghia forms. And in late 1977, there was a 2.3-litre V6 option for the GL and Ghia too.

The counter-balanced tailgate, while not fitted with gas struts to assist opening, led on to a load bay even more commodious than the Mk III's. With the rear seat up, there was 34cu ft of capacity but, with it folded, a massive 64cu ft like a church hall.

There was a load compartment light, albeit one emitting watery illumination, for those winter nights. However, Ford really penny-pinched on the very necessary tailgate wash/wipe system, expecting your hard-pressed old man to fork out extra for it if buying the Base Cortina estate – it was standard on other models.

For families with a large dog or two, this was the Cortina to go for, although well-to-do papas were increasingly drawn to Peugeot and Volvo estates, from which they could gaze at the humble Cortina with disdain. The turncoats.

September 1977

Not generally on sale to the public but devised for bulk sales to fleets is a 1.6-litre Ghia, which rewards employees with luxury yet still maintains low running costs.

The first British six-cylinder Cortina is launched with the new availability of a 108bhp 2293cc V6 engine. It is offered in the GL, S and Ghia models.

Why the Cortina mattered and the Taunus didn't

Did the Taunus have the same special significance to Germany as the Cortina did to Britain? A very subjective issue, of course. Germany has as many automotive icons as we do although, on the world stage, it would be fair to say that the Volkswagen Beetle outdid the Mini, and the Porsche 911 has outshone the Jaguar E-type.

But the 1976 Cortina Mk IV and the contemporary Taunus were actually the same car. There were no significant differences bar two: the 1.3-litre engine option was now confined to British-market cars, and 1.6-, 2.0- and 2.3-litre engines could be had in two-door Taunus form.

The traditional Cortina still had the British market in its usual headlock but, in Germany, buyers were equally well disposed to more advanced products from Volkswagen and Opel. Over there, the Taunus felt out-classed and, indeed, outcast. It wasn't even built in Germany any longer, being assembled instead at Ford's Genk plant in Belgium.

Having said that, both cars were now constructed from bits sourced from across Europe. Carburettors came from Belfast, automatic transmissions from Bordeaux, rear axles from Swansea, Wales and Duren, Germany, engines and panels from all over the place.

But at Dagenham, more components of the Cortina were made on-site than for the Taunus on the other side of the North Sea. Well, that was something to be proud of. Wasn't it? No? Oh, well…

October 1977

The Cortina range is now the widest ever, and prices range from £2523 for a 1300 Base two-door saloon to £4795 for a range-topping 2300 Ghia estate.

September 1978

Inertia reel seat belts are standardised on Base versions.

Never mind the comb-ove
– feel the exhilaration!

The gorgeous Triumph Stag was in its death throes by autumn 1976. It was every dad's idea of a proper four-seater convertible. But not to worry: Ford and Crayford were riding to the rescue.

Crayford's engineers took a leaf out of the Stag's book and adopted its 'T-bar' roof approach for the Cortina Mk IV. The T-shaped steel stiffener linked the car's original B-posts with the windscreen frame for structural rigidity, while extra chassis girders were swathed in sound-deadening foam.

The rear quarter windows were sealed to the hood and disappeared completely when it was lowered. Very Stag, that. Called the SL, a wood dash and stereo radio/cassette were thrown in too.

Crayford was on the case – the £4200 SL was unveiled at the 1976 Earl's Court motor show just one month after the Mk IV itself was launched – and Ford willingly supplied them with big-engined two-door cars from Germany to convert. Your dad was probably salivating slightly at the prospect of getting one from a branch of Bristol Street Motors in Birmingham, Bromley, Cheltenham, Southampton or Worcester…but it was £6545 for a 1.6, and £7485 for a 2.3 V6 by 1979.

In the depths of an economic slump, few were ordered. Crayford sold the project to Carbodies of Coventry in 1980. Only another 30 with fixed rear quarter windows found homes; Ford would launch its own Escort cabriolet in 1984, so the days of these outside chop-tops had passed.

Timeline:
The Ford
Cortina Mk 80

August 1979

Debut of the 'Cortina 80', a thoroughly reworked although outwardly similar car to the Mk IV. It instantly gains the Mk V tag among the British public, which is rather misleading.

Only the rich or foolish drove past the Ford dealer

Ford's industry opposition finally caught up with the Cortina in the late 1970s when the Mk IV was becoming a familiar sight on Britain's roads. Would your dad have been among the many blokes finally ready to consider something – gulp – different?

Of course, it was fine if he was suddenly rolling in it. He could get himself a Ford Granada. Or he could gravitate to one of the 'premium' makes offering a Cortina-sized car, like the Saab 99, BMW 5 Series, Triumph Dolomite or Audi 80. Then, he could afford to cock a snook at the Cortina's decidedly low-tech offering.

For the rest of our fathers, they might have turned Japanese. The latest Datsun Bluebird, Toyota Carina and Mazda 626 were all well-made, rear-drive Cortina clones, and the Honda Accord sedan was an exceptionally good car (if a bit fuddy-duddy).

Renault's 18 of 1978 offered a lot of car for the money, and was briefly popular, although the Fiat Mirafiori, while competent, was tainted with one issue that all dads at the time suspected to be true: cheap Italian cars were crap.

But what if dad's new car still had to be resolutely British at all costs? There was a choice of three. The Morris Marina, and later Ital, could match the Cortina in many area, but its dynamics and image were dire. The Chrysler-Talbot Alpine came with front-wheel drive and a hatchback (the Solara was a conventional saloon spin-off, 1980-on) yet was a 20-watt beacon of mediocrity. And the Vauxhall Cavalier Mk1, in a range that included a couple of tasty coupes but no estate, was at least passably well-made, responsive and stylish. So, that'll be another Cortina, then.

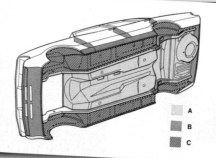

August 1979

Servicing costs are cut with a self-adjusting clutch, maintenance-free wheel bearings, easier brake inspection and new instrument wiring.

A
B
C

August 1979

Cortinas now rust less rapidly thanks to a four-stage anti-corrosion protection regime.

A selection of Cortina Mk IV wannabes, clockwise from below: the Vauxhall Cavalier line-up, the Saab 99, the Renault 18 and the Talbot Solara

August 1979

The sole mechanical change is a power hike for the V6 engine option, which rises to 116bhp.

Zebra 3 in a different sort of Cortina guise

You know the theme tune, you probably remember that Paul Michael Glaser played Starsky and David Soul was Hutch, but can you name the car they screeched around 1970s crime-ridden Bay City in?

It was a Ford Gran Torino – nicknamed "the tomato" and immortalised on the duo's police radio as "Zebra 3" – with a great big white go-faster stripe plastered across its roof and sides and, for when things got tough on a hot tip from Huggy Bear, a flashing roof light that could be attached, by magnet, to the roof.

In 1975, *Starsky & Hutch* wasn't just cool, it was super-cool. Which is more than can be said for this Ford Cortina.

Hastily constructed for Ford's stand at London's first Motorfair in 1977, it boasted wide chrome alloy wheels, a deep front spoiler, wheelarches flared like Hutch's slacks and fake, side-mounted exhaust pipes. And to cash in on *Starsky & Hutch* mania, that distinctive white lightening flash was copied too.

'It demonstrates', claimed Ford, solemnly, 'how the appeal of Britain's best-selling model can be extended way beyond the family car market.' Okay, whatever. It was just a show car and you couldn't buy one. Which is just as well, because seeing an S&H Cortina doing handbrake turns in Fine Fare's car park would surely have shattered our heroes' mystique completely…

Starsky's real Torino was created at the behest of producer Aaron Spelling and, as well as that stripe, featured 'kidney bean' alloy wheels and jacked-up suspension. It's said, on average, one Torino was wrecked for each of the 89 hour-long shows shot between 1975 and '79. *Starsky & Hutch* made its British debut on BBC1 on 30 April 1976.

January 1981

Some £150 is shaved off the price of the Cortina L while an equipment upgrade offers head restraints, a passenger door mirror, a trip mileage recorder and quartz clock. The seat trim is upped to GL spec and a rear centre armrest is chucked in too.

January 1981

Items previously offered as options now become standard at no charge on the Ghia, including a tilt/slide sunroof, electric radio aerial, locking petrol cap, remote control passenger door mirror, sporty gearlever knob. This little lot represents £230-worth of free goodies.

Just when you thought it couldn't get any worse...

You didn't have to be rabidly right-wing to applaud the Conservative landslide at the UK general election of May 1979. Britons of all political persuasions were, after all, in general agreement: the country was on its knees, and had just endured a miserable winter of strikes, short working and power cuts against a backdrop of soaring inflation.

Your dad – all dads – would have despaired at the nation's fate as he supped his Double Diamond at his favourite local. The zealous reforms of 'Thatcherism' were evident as new Prime Minister Maggie got stuck in immediately. Clearly, a lot of people suddenly felt brighter about the future. And the Cortina provided a fascinating barometer of this optimism.

By the end of 1979 the MK IV was already three years old, and was based on a basic design finalised in around 1968. Yet it was to enjoy its best yearly sales ever, with 193,784 new Cortinas licensed for British roads. It took, alone, 11.4% of the total UK new car market.

It must have been havoc at Ford dealers on 1 August, the date when the 'T' registrations officially gave way to the new 'V' plates, as grinning dads picked up their keys, their 12-month warranties, and their brand new Cortinas.

Perhaps it was no surprise that one of the first recipients of Mrs T's big stick was the ailing British Leyland. More than perhaps any other crumbling British institution, here was one organisation that could look to the Ford Cortina, and learn.

April 1981

The limited edition Cortina Carousel is launched; 6000 cars are built in 1.3 and 1.6 forms as saloon and estate, with three two-tone colour schemes offered mixing grey, green and brown in three combos, and 18 trim and equipment upgrades.

A final, and minor, facia/equipment up-grade is made to all models.

"10-4, looks like a convoy of, er, Cortinas, copy?"

Ford had one final trick up its sleeve before it waved goodbye to the Cortina forever in 1982 – a vehicle it hoped would prove just as trustworthy for British buyers.

It was the P100 pick-up, a rakish open-backed truck that originated not from Essex but from thousands of miles away in South Africa. Cortina-based pick-ups had been produced there for yonks, usually from British-made kits with local bodies, but this was the first time the finished product had made the return voyage.

Launched in June 1982, the British-market version had a slightly extended wheelbase so the pick-up bed could cope with the 1-tonne payload that was a feature of popular Japanese equivalents. The engine was the good old petrol 1.6-litre Pinto with a pokey 73bhp, and Ford stressed the transmission package

as though it was something special: 'An 8.5in clutch with four-speed all-synchromesh gearbox'. Would working dads really be impressed by that?

The P100 – and there was not one mention of the Cortina name anywhere on it – was on sale for six years in Britain. It was not a notable hit. This was almost certainly down to the pick-up's build quality. Toyota and Mazda had, for years, been offering similar vehicles where rough edges, indifferent finish and poor ergonomics were not tolerated, and the P100 offered neither a diesel engine nor four-wheel drive.

A second generation P100 used the same conversion trick on the Sierra and, inevitably enough considering Ford's close ties to Mazda, in 1998 the very latest Mazda B1800 appeared in Ford Ranger guise. Sad, that, somehow.

May 1982

The Cortina Crusader is launched as a run-out special edition, although with 30,000 examples built it's virtually a new range edition. Crushed velour on the seats, shiny chrome wheel rim embellishers on sports wheels and – gasp – a remote-control driver's door mirror.

The Cortina 80 ends manufacture at Dagenham, after 20 years of continuous Cortina production there

Tributes rain down on 'the Cortina: cultural icon'

The Cortina became so much a part of the collective national consciousness that it was treated to a memorable hour-long BBC *Arena* documentary upon its 1982 demise.

Called *The Private Life of the Ford Cortina*, it was hosted by Alexei Sayle, the Liverpool 'alternative' comedian who'd shot to fame in cult BBC2 sit-com *The Young Ones*.

In an interview with former bank robber John McVicar, the Cortina was eulogised as an excellent getaway car. The Poet Laureate, Sir John Betjeman, was featured because he once included the Cortina in a satirical poem about 'Executives'. Tom Robinson, the rocker behind the song *2-4-6-8 Motorway* was another talking head while 'typical' owners, possibly a bit like your dad, were also interviewed.

It's since been dubbed: 'A history of Britain's most popular, most stolen and most misunderstood car'.

Alexei Sayle cashed in further with his offbeat 1982 single *Ullo John! Gotta New Motor?* Re-released two years later, it got to No 15 in the charts, and Sayle made his bizarrely jerky debut on *Top of the Pops*. The deranged lyrics were totally unfathomable. Here's a snatch from verse two:

Ullo John! Gotta new motor?
Ullo John! Gotta new motor?
They put me in a special hospital.
Is there life on Mars?
Is there life in Peckham?
What's that sicko there for?
Ah ah ah ah ow…ah ah ah ah ow [monkey sounds]

September 1982

Launch of the Ford Sierra creates a media storm…but the Ford dealer network is still stuffed with new Cortinas – the final nine examples, amazingly, aren't actually sold until 1987!

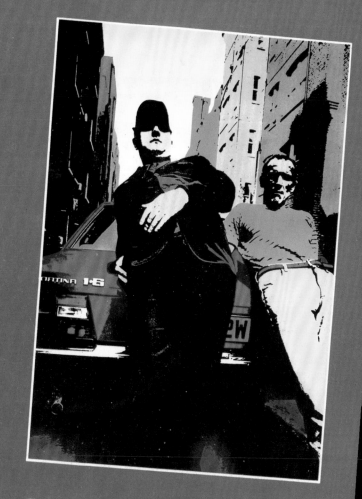

ALEXEI SAYLE

'ULLO JOHN! GOTTA NEW MOTOR?

The last CORTINA
1962-1982

Cortina runs out of road

In September 1979, the final chapter in the Cortina saga began with a rather surprising move from Ford. Dads everywhere temporarily forgot about the dire state of the British economy and the recent 'winter of discontent' with its strikes and power cuts, and did a double-take.

Yet another new series was proudly presented under the banner of 'Cortina 80'. The car appeared indistinguishable from the outgoing car; yet in reality the transformation was almost as thorough as the metamorphosis of Mk III into Mk IV.

For although the car used basically Mk III running gear once again, the Cortina 80 had been rebodied while adhering closely to the Mk IV profile. You'd have to study the Mk IV and the 80 closely side by side to spot the differences, but in fact every panel had been subtly altered. The most obvious change was to the doors, which now had taller glass areas extending further upwards into a roof that had a much flatter, less domed shape. The windscreen was taller too. The front grille was wider, the front spoiler was deeper, there were huge new rear light clusters, and the bumpers now extended around the corners of the car to meet the wheelarches.

Engines were improved, to make them both more powerful and more thrifty. All units now had a viscous-coupled thermostatic fan to improve economy and quietness, while the 1.3- and 1.6-litre benefited from variable-venturi carburettors for better 'breathing'.

Inside, your dad would have been impressed by the trendy open-framed headrests, the new side window demisting facility, and the new sprung-platform construction and infinitely-variable backrest that made the front seats so much more comfy.

The Cortina 80 range, which started at £3346, was as comprehensive as ever, spanning five different power units from a 61bhp 1.3-litre to a

Opposite: Dagenham's historic day; below: the Cortina 80's dozen top draws

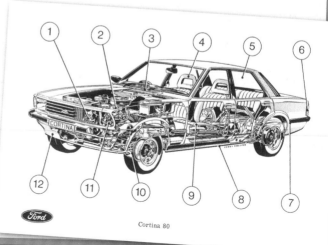

Cortina 80

116bhp 2.3, variously offered in two-door saloon, four-door saloon and five-door estate formats. Trim levels offered included Base, L, GL and Ghia. The familiar mix-and-match approach made for a bewildering choice of 20 models, but that was before you factored in special equipment packs. Confirming the Cortina's latterday role as a simple family car, the S model had been axed, but an 'S' wheel/suspension package could now be ordered for any model, as could a 'heavy duty' package that beefed up the driveline for Cortinas likely to be used as cargo-haulers, towcars or on farms or building sites. Ford also produced a special two-door Base 1.6 automatic for exclusive sale to disabled drivers through Motability schemes. Plus, there was great news for DIY dads: service intervals had been stretched to every 6000 miles!

Below: the full gamut of Cortina 80s, with a GLS and a Ghia out front

Every base seemed to be covered, but there was no escaping the fact that the Cortina was an ageing concept, and Ford executives willingly admitted this would be the last of the line. Aficionados, however, quickly named it the Mk V (never its official title, it must be said), and the fact that the Cortina, perhaps unbeknown to many a proud dad leathering the final drops of water off his gleaming example of a Sunday morning, was yesterday's car seemed to barely effect sales.

Fie to new technology, aerodynamics and electronic gadgetry! The humble Cortina 80 was the best-selling car in Britain in 1981. This meant Cortinas had been your country's favourite motor for virtually a full decade from 1972 to 1981, beaten into second place only in 1976 when the Ford Escort outsold it by 7621 units, and again in 1982.

It was an irony that, truly in its twilight years, the Cortina saw its best month ever for British sales in August 1981, when an absurdly enormous 25,790 were driven away from dealers. And showroom interest was further boosted in 1981 and '82 by two limited editions. First came the 6000-off Cortina Carousel, swiftly followed by the Cortina Crusader. 'Impressive livery, impressive pedigree', boasted Ford...although you had to pay extra for a two-tone paintjob in blue or red over silver and, with 30,000 cars built, it was hardly exclusive.

The inevitable but sad end came on 22 July 1982, when the final Cortina came down the Dagenham production line. Ford ensured it would never build another car like it by immediately launching the Sierra as its replacement. British suburbia was collectively mortified by the sight of this plasticky jellymould, and the goodwill so painstakingly built up over the last two decades by the Cortina began to evaporate like an autumn mist.

Trad dads across the British Isles started to do the unthinkable, and consider a car from another manufacturer. The Vauxhall Cavalier was the main beneficiary of their interest, especially after a diesel model was offered. Two years later, the Austin Montego was picking up significant numbers of disgruntled Cortina folk too. And, once accustomed to the startling shape of the Sierra, buyers were apt to feel more adventurous and consider even more radical options; hence, the Citroen BX proved a phenomenally successful car in Britain. Who'd have thought it…

Speaking in 2002, the then chairman of Ford Motor Company Ltd, Roger Putnam, longingly summed up the Cortina's importance to the company:

"The popularity of the Cortina throughout its lifetime is confirmed by the amazing sales statistics of the period. In its best sales year ever, 1979, just under 194,000 Cortinas were sold in Britain."

That year, the Mk IV/Cortina 80 had 11.3% of the British market to itself. And here's some more great statistics:

When the Sierra (above) arrived in 1982, the Cortina 80 suddenly seemed very old hat indeed

The Cortina was Britain's best-selling car for 10 of the 20 years it was on sale: 1967, 1972, 1973, 1974, 1975, 1977, 1978, 1979, 1980, 1981. It was in second place for eight years and in third for the remaining two.

Total production of all Cortinas was 4,279,079, of which 3,155,161 cars were built at Dagenham. From the balance, 788,012 were supplied as kits for assembly in other countries. They were shipped in what the car industry calls CKD form, standing for 'completely knocked down' to plants in Genk (Belgium), Amsterdam, Cork (Ireland), Victoria (Australia), Port Elizabeth (South Africa) and also, in the case of the Lotus-Cortina Mk1, just up the road to Cheshunt.

Cortina production and sales figures

Production of the four Cortina Marks

Mk I, 1962–66 1,013,391	Mk III, 1970–76 1,126,559
Mk II, 1966–70 1,024,869	Mk IV & '80', 1976–82 1,131,850

Cortina sales to British Dads (mostly)

1962 17,345	**1971** 102,214	**1980** 190,281
1963 109,478	**1972** 187,159	**1981** 159,804
1964 117,250	**1973** 181,641	**1982** 135,745
1965 116,637	**1974** 131,280	**1983** 11,598
1966 127,039	**1975** 106,837	**1984** 139
1967 165,123	**1976** 126,263	**1985** 68
1968 137,636	**1977** 120,601	**1986** 62
1969 116,186	**1978** 139,204	**1987** 9
1970 123,256	**1979** 193,784	Grand Total 2,816,639